Remem

~ AT TIME'S EDGE ~

*Remembering
Anne Cluysenaar*

Published by
The Vaughan Association

© Copyright remains with the author

Published in 2016
Published by The Vaughan Association

*All rights reserved. No part of this publication maybe
reproduced, stored in a retrieval system,
or transmitted, in any form or by any means,
electronic, mechanical, photocopying, recording
or otherwise, without the prior permission of
The Vaughan Association.*

ISBN 13: 978-1530222452
ISBN 10: 1530222451

Published with the generous financial support of those who loved and remembered Anne.

Edited by Fiona Owen

General Editor: Dr. Joseph Sterrett

Editorial Board:
Prof. Alan Rudrum
Prof. Donald Dickson
Prof. Helen Wilcox
Dr. Robert Wilcher

Advisors:
John Barnie, Robert Minhinnick
Prof. M. Wynn Thomas

Typeset by Dinefwr Press
Rawlings Road, Llandybïe, Carmarthenshire, SA18 3YD
Printed by CreateSpace, USA

Dedicated to our friend
Anne Cluysenaar
(1936-2014)
'a true poet'

Photo by John Briggs, with kind permission.

Contents

Preface   9

Ruth Bidgood	One Day (for Anne)	13
Philip Gross	Written on Light	14
Jeremy Hooker	At Time's Edge	16
Jan Fortune	A Tribute to Anne Cluysenaar	19
Dave Ward	Anne Cluysenaar	22
Bob Wilcher	Reflection	23
Wendy Mulford	The Stone	26
Meredith Andrea	Etching	27
Alison Brackenbury	January	28
Rose Flint	Poetry Book	29
Christopher Meredith	Standing Place	30
Helen and Allan Wilcox	Anne Cluysenaar at Birmingham	32
Ann Drysdale	For Anne, from Ann	35
Paul Matthews	Far Off	39
	Gathering Nectar	39
	Writing Among Animals	40
Seán Street	Fieldfares	41
Ric Hool	Incantation	42
Myra Schneider	His Gift from Brazil	43
	The First of Spring	44
Charles Wilkinson	Reflections on Anne Cluysenaar at Lancaster and in Wales	46
Mary MacGregor	Siluria Siluriensis	50
Norman Schwenk	Quintet for Anne	51
David Hart	I imagined	52
Neil Curry	The Well	53
Helen Moore	Deep Time, Deep Tissue	54
John Killick	Sequences in the Poetry of Anne Cluysenaar	57
Jeremy Hilton	from a Derbyshire sequence	64
Colin Moss	The Sheaves of Day	67

Roger Hubank	Anne Cluysenaar	71
Patricia McCarthy	In Dublin's Fair City	75
Jay Ramsay	Scintilla	77
Dilys Wood	Anne in Dulwich	78
Graham Hartill	from Migrating Bones	81
Frank Olding	Rhiannon (English)	84
	Rhiannon (Welsh)	86
Tony Curtis	Following the Horses	88
Stevie Davies	Henry Vaughan, Edward Lhuyd, Anne Cluysenaar & and Stones	89
Hilary Llewellyn-Williams	Like Them that Dream	94
John Freeman	Time Perpetually Revolving	97
David Grubb	Astonishings	103
Stevie Krayer	You Have One Missed Message	104
John Barnie	Evening in Winter	105
	Happiness	105
Kate Foley	For Anne Cluysenaar	107
Hilary Davies	By the Dark Lake	108
John Powell Ward	Bereavement	109
Susan Bassnett	Living on in Life-Praise	110
Bonnie Thurston	A Poet, a Theologian and a Rabbit ('for us, metaphorical'): A Reminiscence and Two Poems	117
	Broaching Distances	121

Graham Harris – Anne's Plaque 122
Contributors, Acknowledgements and Permissions 123
The Artist 130
The Photographer 130

Preface

There is no knowing, in any life, what is to come in the twists and turns along the way, and though we all know that death will find each of us, the hour and means remains mercifully hidden. Anne Cluysenaar's death on November 1st 2014 shocked us all. How she died is public knowledge and I won't dwell on it here. Suffice to say that grief has had its due place in the process of bringing this memorial volume together – for myself and the contributors. However, what comes in these pages is as much a celebration and affirmation of the person and poet that Anne was, and is testament to her ability to touch deeply into the lives of so many of us.

Anne's death occurred just two months after the passing of Peter Thomas, who had been suffering with cancer. In the life of the Vaughan Association and *Scintilla*, its journal, this was, then, a most tragic year. It was Peter and Anne who founded the Association in the late 1990s. They set up the colloquia and edited *Scintilla* from its inception. As Helen and Allan Wilcox write within, Anne and Peter 'fulfilled a vision of the partnership between creativity and scholarship in the service of the Vaughans, Welsh writing, new poetry, visual art, spirituality and the natural world'. The first edition of *Scintilla* was published in 1997, with Anne as general editor. By the third issue, the editorial team that would last until 2011 was in place, with Peter at the helm as general editor, and Anne working with Graham Hartill and Hilary Llewellyn-Williams as poetry editors.

I met Anne and Peter when I attended my first colloquium in the late 1990s. It was held in that grand place, Buckland Hall, near the river Usk. I remember its sweeping staircase and mighty chestnut trees. I felt like a slip of a girl in that company of elders, yet when hazarding a small comment during a discussion, Anne later drew on it. Here was this eminent woman, who so impressed me, 'liking what I'd said', drawing me into deeper conversation. In the poems, essays, reflections and reminiscings in this volume, this is one of the qualities that others so often speak of. Anne had that rare gift of drawing out the best in people. She cared. She was interested in others. She paid, as John Freeman puts it, 'palpable attention, you could feel'.

Most people included in this volume have known Anne personally, in some cases across many decades. This means that vivid snapshots of Anne's life emerge: Anne at Dilys Wood's house in Dulwich, 'in the back bedroom, tea tray before her, a large cashmere shawl . . . round her shoulders'; Anne with Ruth Bidgood over a pub lunch where 'there were stories / of your animals at home, of doves / you would write about'; Anne in Monmouth with Bonnie Thurston and the touching encounter with a rabbit.

We hear, from former students and colleagues, about Anne's teaching life in the universities of Lancaster, Birmingham and Cardiff. Anne was clearly an inspiring tutor. Lancaster University during the early 1970s was, according to Dave Ward, 'an intoxicating environment . . . a heady mix of Adrian Mitchell's Song Workshop, Lancaster Street Theatre, the Socialist Society ('Soc Soc'), poetry readings, protests, rock bands and multi-media events. And there was Anne, in the middle of it all, always smiling, always friendly, encouraging and supportive'. Charles Wilkinson describes how Anne was one of 'two members of faculty to whom young poets would show their work . . . both generous with their time and unfailingly courteous to students'.

Helen and Allan Wilcox first met Anne when she was a young lecturer. They were her students at Birmingham University, and remember the impact she made on them: 'her austere beauty and elegance, her commitment to new and unfamiliar subjects such as stylistics and creative writing, and above all her slow and steady articulation of spoken English in an accent mysteriously coloured by the foreign contexts in which she had grown up'. They 'were intrigued, and not a little awed, by her'.

'Awe' is also something Normal Schwenk mentions about Anne as a colleague, in a haiku from his 'Quintet':

> We were a little
> in awe of you, I believe:
> you stuck to your guns

and in his biographical note, he describes bringing Anne to Cardiff University to teach on the new postgraduate Creative Writing programme in the early 1990s as 'one of his proudest achievements'.

When Anne moved to Wales with her beloved husband of thirty-nine years, Walt, she found, in Little Wentworth Farm, a home and *locus* out of which she wrote some of her finest poetry, and where she was inspired by other writers of that area, most notably Henry Vaughan and Alfred Russel Wallace. Throughout her collections, the trickle of names can be found – dedications to friends, alive and dead, the marking of rites, poetry as conversation, a reach through time. As Stevie Davies writes, 'She had an extraordinary gift for friendship'. And what becomes increasingly evident from the pieces in this volume is Anne's keen interest, her polymathic curiosity. Susan Bassnett, who was Anne's close friend for forty years, as well as her Executor and Literary Executor, writes movingly of packing away Anne's books after her death: 'the sheer range of subjects combined with the evidence of how carefully those books had been read, the handwritten marginalia, the endless tiny scraps of paper marking topics and pages, the notes pushed in between pages. Anne was an intellectual omnivore, and her books span the arts, humanities and sciences'. Bob Wilcher notes similarly Anne's 'tireless range of interests', with geology, one year, becoming 'a particular source of inspiration for her . . . [she] was the person one turned to for new depths of insight into what it means to be both a thinking and feeling human being and a part of the natural world.'

This range of interests can be seen in Anne's writing and, most notably, in her poetry, that great legacy, where her voice now abides – and it isn't just *range* we experience in her writing, but *depth*. She had such an ability to attend, to *be with*, to notice, as Charles Wilkinson puts it, 'the minutiae that would pass unremarked by a less observant witness – the subtle shifting of light in a valley, a wasps' nest, petals, a hoof print'. Anne shared with both Vaughan and Wallace a deep connection with the natural world and, as Roger Hubank notes, hers was a 'felt kinship with creation in all its particularity' – her cat, her sheep, her horse, her bantam, these loved creatures could prompt her into meditation no less than a chance encounter with a blackbird, spider or bee.

We see, in poem after poem, the way Anne's experience is translated and transformed into poetry; it is what Stevie Davies calls 'the unique empathy and honesty of her poesis' that distinguishes Anne's work and makes her, as Jeremy Hooker puts it, a 'true poet'. Indeed, we can apply to herself the line that Anne writes of Vaughan in her introduction to *Henry Vaughan: Selected Poems*: that '"my heart, my verse" must be as one'. That is certainly borne out in her work, where she finds a consistently personal voice for her final collection of diary poems, *Touching Distances*.

Roger Hubank reminds us that, for Anne, 'a true poem . . . is analogous to mystical experience. It takes place in an inner room, a place towards which language points but can never reach'. Anne's 'sensibility', he writes, 'was essentially religious, wholly and seriously alert to life in a way rarely observed in others. For her what we call "mystery" was not a problem to be explained away; not something that surrounds whatever it is – a sort of invisible shell – but the thing itself'.

Late in life, in 2012, Anne became a Quaker. She could never – as she wrote to me in an email – 'toe doctrinal lines', but with the openness of Friends, the silent worship and notion of Inner Light, she found herself spiritually at home. We had email conversations as she grew towards membership and then, one morning, an email popped into my inbox saying simply: 'Ah! I am a Quaker!' It is pertinent, therefore, that 'light' flickers among these pages, as in Phillip Gross's 'Written on Light', where we are, finally,

> held
> gently and exactly.
> Held up, to be filled with light.

Anne, of course, wrote about death. In her final two collections, there is an almost foreseeing quality to some of the poems. Anne was the very best of wonderers and she probed deeply into the mysterious business of being here. Her reach was through deep time and in poems like 'I remember this much. The sun' and 'There were dark leaves spread out' (*Migrations*), she describes unitive experiences that many would call mystical. The last poem of the last book, *Touching Distances*, ends in winter, where Anne describes herself 'sowing wildflower seeds' for a future 'lost sight of'. The final lines bring a 'flurry of snow' . . . yet the cold is 'generative'.

It has been a great privilege to work on bringing these remarkable pieces of writing together, in Anne's name. I would like to thank *Scintilla's* general editor, Joseph Sterrett, for inviting me to undertake this (albeit daunting) task. Anne was widely known and loved, so, despite my best efforts, there may be some significant gaps – missing people – among these pages, for which I give my sincere apologies.

I would like to thank Ric Hool for his help with the two photographs included. At the eleventh hour, he located the beautiful photograph of Anne printed here, along with the photographer, John Briggs, who went on to kindly grant us permission to include it.

The images used are by the Eastbourne artist, and Quaker, Ann Johnson, whose work Anne admired. Ann's sketches have touched so perfectly into the pieces gathered here, not merely decorating the issue but deepening it. My warmest thanks to her.

Thanks to all those who donated to this publication, and, of course, to the contributors themselves who have, between them, created such a fitting memorial to Anne. The title is from Jeremy Hooker's sequence, with warm thanks to him; also to Jan Fortune, of Cinnamon Press.

And so, then, I finish with poetry. May these lines serve as a blessing for Anne. They are from a poem within, by Paul Matthews, and echo what Susan Bassnett writes, herself echoing Anne, that 'there is death, but there is also the everlasting renewal of matter':

>All flesh is grass.
>This flowering
>
>meadow (mowed
>and mowed again)
>
>returns abundantly.
>Sweet clover, testify.
>
>What other evidence
>than love is needed.

Fiona Owen
February 2016

RUTH BIDGOOD

One Day (for Anne)

Could death unmake
a day made so well?
I have not thought so.

Opening the album again, I see,
as it was then, the two of us, friends
not in the picture, but there, our eyes
delighting in what the camera saved,
surge of a field, promise of budded boughs,
line of hills beyond.

Over pub lunch there were stories
of your animals at home, of doves
you would write about. And lightly
ideas crossed the table, to and fro – a sharing
of your profundities, laughter, questions,
warmth, serenity. Something
was made, and would last.

It is with me now as we stand
out of frame, savouring
the brink of spring, perhaps both
having some notion of endlessness
hidden in a carefree day.

PHILIP GROSS

Written on Light

Beyond the pier this morning,
a pure dazzle – only, in it, silently,

the come and go of white sails,
right to left and left to right,

translucent, barely distinct
from the depthlessness they move in

– slight geometries and intersections
of it in the stillness, just perceptibly

filling or flexing. Beyond our gravity
there are craft (there are, already)

that ride on the breath of the sun,
the mere pressure of light.

*

   Just come
into its own, the day,
   the twice –
times sun, the sum

of suns, it and its own
   reflection
on the sea. Its self –
   sufficiency.

*

Such a delicate cusp
this evening: the sky,
the sea
       and the barely
discernible hinge between them.

No, I don't believe
in Judgement but yes,
we will be held
       to account.
Like this. In every detail.

Held, that is, as in a rare
find, fine china, the one of itself,
with its flaws, held
       gently and exactly.
Held up, to be filled with light

JEREMY HOOKER

At Time's Edge

In memory of Anne Cluysenaar

1
Seeking words to speak of you
I hear you say: *'where
we are both strangers and at home'*.

I respond, and expect you to answer.
I listen, and the silence, like a sea
gone far out, reverberates
leadenly with a memory of sound.

> *Fire lips
> water
> as the day dies*

2
Searching for news of you
I stumble on a photograph
taken in a Somerset farmyard:
Ministry of Information, 1944.

You are standing with your parents,
artists in exile. A donkey
is nuzzling your father's hand.
A goose and a hen pick in the mud
around your feet.
How solid you are,
what a sturdy little girl
with a mass of blond hair:
the poet at nine years of age.

> *Fire quickens
> touching
> the water's skin*

3
It is the moment that holds you
and where you are, in wartime
at this English farm, you are
in a place no one can see:
                a border
between languages and countries.
At this edge, you are
already, in your way, the stranger
you taught me, in my way, to know myself.

            Blood-lipped
            a wave seethes
            kissing the shore

4
Dare I speak aloud
what I say to myself:
dear soul, dear fellow pilgrim?

Will the language we hear
around us bear such words?

'If breath is not spirit,
what is it for?'
I hear you ask.

            Snakes of fire
            ride in
            with the tide

5
What I see is you
with your whole life –
not finished, but like a sea
that has heaved up against a wall.

It is the self you knew as process:
tides, currents, depths.
And in the depths life glimpsed
or unknown, but generative,
the creative source you knew as a child.

> *Water covers prints*
> *first light*
> *will expose*

6
Wales became your home,
the depth of time exposed
in rock fall and quarry face,
the first footprint on an ancient beach,
the labyrinthine forest paths
and sheep walks, ways
of poet and healer, and ever
the green and shadowed places
of Wentwood Forest, the Beacons
and Black Mountains
and valley of the river Usk.

It became your home
because you did not claim it,
but knew yourself a wanderer
in and out of languages, and between
countries, along the edge of time.

> *The night,*
> *the black night,*
> *shivers with stars*

7
A true poet, your life is still to come
in other minds: the life embodied
in your words, a life's work,
quick and shining, which helps
other strangers to know themselves.

A Tribute to Anne Cluysenaar, 1936-2014

JAN FORTUNE

I was staying with friends on November 2nd, after a lovely Cinnamon book launch, when I received a very sad email from one of our poets, telling me about Anne's sudden death. I was shocked and confused, especially when I read on and discovered that Anne had been killed, that here stepson was in custody and her husband in hospital.

It is terrible for anyone to die violently and it seemed particularly so in the case of someone so gracious, intelligent, lively and generous. Recently Anne was thrilled that The Charlier Museum in Brussels put on a five generation retrospective of the work of the Cluysenaar family – from her architect great-great-grandfather Jean-Pierre down through her great-grandfather, Alfred, a sculptor, her grandfather, André, a painter, and her father John, also a painter and ending with poetic work by Anne. She was also excited to be working with Geoff Palmer, a talented musician, setting some of the diary poems to music. This was a poet with so much still to give and a person who cared deeply – about family, friends, language, her art; about life.

Cinnamon published the last two of Anne's collections and she's also championed the poetry of several other Cinnamon authors so I'd worked with Anne closely over the last few years. She was always a delight to work with – sharp-eyed, meticulous, a person of integrity and loyalty, and also someone who was warm and humane. She had just sent me the kernel of her next manuscript – 17 beautifully honed, lucid poems with themes around childhood, art, love, war, culture, deep time . . . As Anne said in her email to me, 'What else?' The only answer to that now is that the unpublished work must find its way into the world – the last of her extraordinary writing that read so simply, so elegantly, but always brought great pressure to bear on every word.

Many tributes have been paid. Gwyneth Lewis, writing in *The Sunday Times*, noted, 'In Anne's company, I felt that being a poet was the most natural thing in the world.' Jeremy Hooker, writing in *Poetry Wales*, has said that Anne was 'one of the finest poets of our time' and that her late poems showed her 'at the height of her powers'. I can only concur. It was a privilege to know

Anne, as her editor and as her friend. I'm proud that Cinnamon's list includes her final two collections, testaments to her clear-sighted curiosity, precision and empathy, and hope that a final work is still to come.

From *Migrations*:

World

for Myra Schneider

What would we do without world?
We don't even know what we feel,
what we think, till something out there
catches our eye and draws

a response from the darkness inside,
fills it with places to live in –
streams and trees and flowers
with their own ways of being.

And of course not only good things
come. But among them the loved
faces, those eyes within which
other worlds wait to explore us.

There might be a gesture, a word not
spoken, or a word, or a touch
which we shut our eyes to receive.
What was outside may become then

more of self than our cells helplessly
growing or dying or changing.
One world will open to another.
Through echoes. Through transformations.

REFLECTION

From *Touching Distances:*

January 8

On receiving from Michael Srigley a letter about 'Crossings, xxxvi'
in Seamus Heaney's Seeing Things

Seeing things, and seeing things, that night
when the car dipped underfoot and a phrase from Dante
came to him, about fireflies, clearing his head,
and policemen's torches searched the distance behind.

But still the dark of his own night-crossing to come,
its plain reality darker than any poem . . .
Voices of ghosts once as real as he is – poets
in dangerous times long gone – steady the present.

And an almost lifelong friend reminds me now
by letter how the dead may come to us still
or we cross over to them through depths of being
which words help us find as we dare our little boat.

Virgil describes a wave shuddering in darkness,
a wave he must, some night, have seen and felt.
We will never know about that. But our own time,
evanescent as his, steadies, hearing his voice.

Anne Cluysenaar

DAVE WARD

Anne Cluysenaar sat in her small office in the newly-built, gleaming white campus on top of the drafty hill. Her door was open as she spoke excitedly on the telephone to her publisher about the proofs of her first pamphlet collection *Nodes*.

Lancaster University was an intoxicating environment as the late Sixties nudged into the early Seventies: a heady mix of Adrian Mitchell's Song Workshop, Lancaster Street Theatre, the Socialist Society ('Soc Soc'), poetry readings, protests, rock bands and multi-media events. And there was Anne, in the middle of it all, always smiling, always friendly, encouraging and supportive, with the ever-open door when I needed to go to her – very concerned that *Continuum*, the arts magazine which I had taken over from Derek Noonan, hadn't achieved its expected sales. She explained that the new austere white cover that we'd gone for was a mistake. 'White is not a selling colour,' she said. We soon put that right with the next issue.

In seminars there was the same steady patience, though more than once she could be distracted into a debate about *Monty Python's Flying Circus!*

Then another open-door moment. Ann was excitedly brushing her hair. 'We've got a meeting with the head of department,' she confided – followed later by the delighted news that 'We got it!' She and David Craig would be setting up the first accredited Creative Writing module in a British university.

Those sessions felt very special. There was an atmosphere of trail-blazing, of going into the unknown. A small cluster of students, all of us already writing, were given free rein to read and discuss each other's work, along with Anne and David – themselves established writers. We were guided, we were encouraged, we were empowered – but never felt that we were being instructed or handed formulaic approaches.

I treasure those years, and remembering Anne, realise that it was the best foundation an aspiring writer could have had.

Reflection

BOB WILCHER

I first met Anne during the 1970s, when she joined the Language staff in the Department of English Language and Literature at the University of Birmingham and settled into the room opposite mine on the 'English corridor'. We soon discovered that we had interests in common when she became supervisor of a postgraduate student, whose MA thesis on Thom Gunn I had overseen a few years before. When she left for a post in Sheffield, I took over supervision of his thesis, which was on Landscape and Modern Poetry and included a chapter on the work of Jeremy Hooker. Many years later, when I began to attend the Vaughan Colloquium at the end of the 1990s, it was a great pleasure to pick up the threads of my acquaintance with Anne and to discover that another regular participant was none other than Jerry Hooker himself. Each April from then on, one of the delights that Miriam and I looked forward to was catching up with the last year's news over a cup of tea with Anne – and consolidating our friendship over a glass or two of something stronger, often in conversations that went on until most people had retired for the night. One of the pleasant surprises of getting older is that one discovers there is so much still to learn, and every year Anne, with her tireless range of interests – geology, I learned one year, had become a particular source of inspiration for her – was the person one turned to for new depths of insight into what it means to be both a thinking and feeling human being and a part of the natural world. We shall miss her quiet but uncompromising devotion to the rigours of the art of poetry and the many serious concerns that it encompassed.

The Downs above Malborough

Up where the track of prehistoric men
Crosses the downs from fort to fort
And growing things reach
Through a soil that's sharp with flints
Stand sarsen stones

Abrupt and hard
Against the wavering line where hill meets sky.
Such things survive according to their kind.
Downland grass and flowers
Rooting and rotting in the earth
Reiterate in endless sequence what they are
While rock's more stubborn emphasis
Outlasts the changing contour of the hills.

July 2015

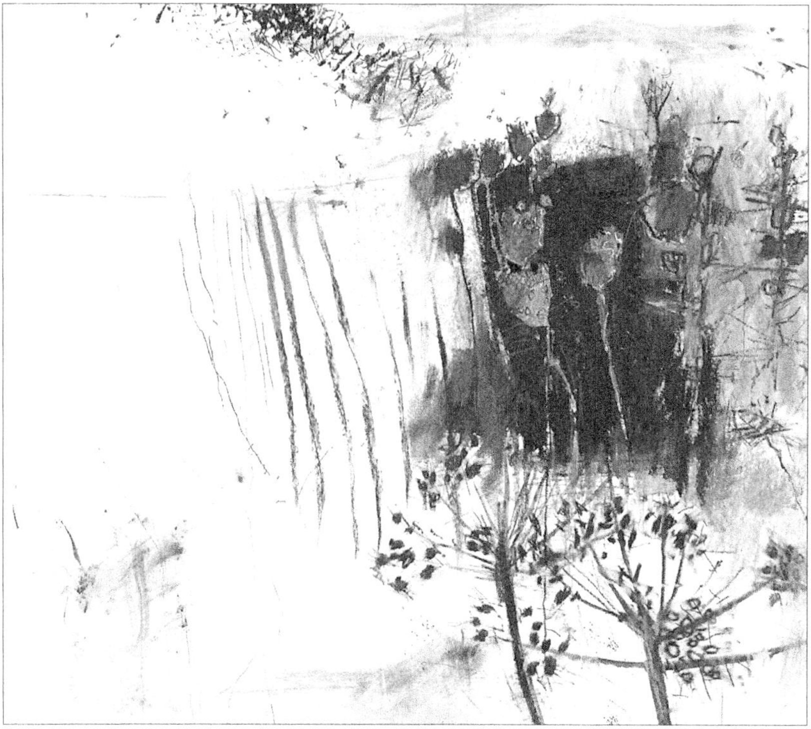

WENDY MULFORD

The Stone:

it sits among the old concerns
sky   blue   savage
if here there were a hill to carve
I could believe it –

'*when God calls me/*
                              by name/
I am/
          earth   air   water   flame'

Caithness flagstone bird-bath bowl. Around the rim, lettering in 'Norn', the ancient Orkney language: 'Give us this day our daily bread'. Quotation from Robert Rendall (20th century Orkney poet).

MEREDITH ANDREA

Etching

To Anne

The train slows and nearing the border, snow
whites out fields,
the outline of hills.

Trees are ink pools
clotted in rooks' nests in birch;
fences gouged to hold field to field.

From under a black cloud-ledge light is breaking,
a gloria of cold fire igniting rust
in the iron barn, fields flashing
where the river's broken.

It means. I feel it,
but can't explain; that cottage
open to the elements –
charred roof-beams, tumbled stone.

You tell me, in memory, to *observe* the path
that leads there, goes past it, on

through birchwoods, to a field of sky.

ALISON BRACKENBURY

January

Harsh, hateful month, yet morning's moon,
my silver penny, dear as dark,
floods ash buds black, as first cars fume.
For January brings work, work, work.
Have you heard the town foxes bark?
How screams as sharp as yours or mine,
hungry and raw as children, spark
our small rooms by the railway line?

Work ends.　Dusk drops.　I tramp from car,
call my old horse. Wreathed hill mists pass.
Our heated world already stars
daisies across the hoof-pocked grass.
The rescued mare, found fly-grazed, thin,
now trots with Christmas foal at heels.
A few days old, or thirty springs,
all charge for stables, leave night's fields.

Out January's dark and freezing rain
I reach my kitchen's warm cocoon.
I dream of my grandmother's pudding,
hot steamed sponge sliding from the spoon
with dripping amber, her plum jam,
lost summer caught, red in jars' rank.
She fed her neighbour's hungry son,
I find tinned beans for a food bank.

Are you in your warm kitchen now?
Keep off the killing New Year's dark
which has drunk some we love, but how
in mud, in rooms, we make our mark.
Peel the potatoes.　Stir the spoon.
I hope, before lit days, and many,
you meet a January moon.
How will you spend your silver penny?

ROSE FLINT

Poetry Book

Today, the girl in the shop
sold me your poems
with such tenderness
her hand folding
carefully around the cover

as if she touched sheet gold
sheer, untextured
by cold February weather

I could have requested packaging
but I am a Green and have no need
unless it would have been to stay
the moment of her smile

against my loneliness
her hand folding, gentle wrapping
of exchange.

She wanted me to love your book
not knowing that I did already
your lines in my mind
her hand folding
your tenderness   as if pouring
pouring a pitcher of sunlight into me.

CHRISTOPHER MEREDITH

Standing place

Stanza: Italian, 'standing place'

When you step in to the empty room
you interrupt whatever it was
that the room wasn't doing

you break the calm
of the lucid glass
on a lonely lake
and it rocks
and a wave refracts across
let's say

the rug on a pinewood floor
and ruffles the solid fireplace

and the table shakes

the sculpted teapot still as de Chirico
does a jelly shiver
and resets

the frozen desklamp
melts and lists

the windowglass becomes
its own blown curtain
and the garden outside billows
and settles

the sofa starts from its doze
and lifts a head and stares at
where you seem to be.

And if you're smart
you pause just one step in
and slowly lower the foot you've raised
arms out for balance
and you barely move
as you barely breathe
and you stand
try
teetering
to meet
the stillness of the pool
become the statue in an empty square.

But you are the blurs on the street
in early photographs
the ghost in the room
the solid room that barely senses you
in this glass shudder.

This is the standing place
where you can't stay
the still lake in the dream of trees
doing still
the thing it does not do.
These are the words telling nothing
that are there before
and after you.

Anne Cluysenaar at Birmingham

HELEN AND ALLAN WILCOX

(with thanks to Phil Herbert, Elaine Hobby, Clare Shirtcliff and other fellow-students of English at Birmingham in the 1970s)

It was a relatively recent pleasure for us to get to know Anne and build up a friendship through the Vaughan Association. We greatly enjoyed the privilege of meeting her regularly at the colloquium from 2006 onwards, after we moved to Wales from the Netherlands. We took delight each year in hearing Anne read her latest, deftly expressive poems, and we benefited enormously from the sustained wisdom of her responses to other people's talks and readings. The unostentatious, informal yet intensely inspiring atmosphere of the colloquia undoubtedly owed a great deal to Anne's personality, in an ideal combination with Peter's unruffled organisational manner and quiet, ironic determination. Together they fulfilled a vision of the partnership between creativity and scholarship in the service of the Vaughans, Welsh writing, new poetry, visual art, spirituality and the natural world. That Anne and Peter should die within a few months of each other is a profound loss to all who knew them and to the society and journal they founded.

Our original connection with Anne, however, dates back a lot further than the Usk Valley Vaughan Association, to the mid-1970s and the far less pastoral context of the industrial West Midlands. We were students of English at Birmingham University when Anne was a young lecturer in our department. We remember the impact she made on us then: her austere beauty and elegance, her commitment to new and unfamiliar subjects such as stylistics and creative writing, and above all her slow and steady articulation of spoken English in an accent mysteriously coloured by the foreign contexts in which she had grown up. We were intrigued, and not a little awed, by her. Unlike all our other lecturers, she invited us to call her by her first name, marking her out as radically informal and someone in whom we could confide, though there was still always a slight distance between her and ourselves, a mixture of respect and self-preservation.

One of our fellow students remembers that, at the end of her first year of studying English at Birmingham, she was feeling uncertain about whether to stay on at university – so she chose to go and knock on Anne's door. Despite the fact that Anne had not been her tutor during the first year, our friend was sure that this was the right person with whom to speak about her dilemma. It was a matter of trust: she somehow knew that Anne would listen calmly and not intrude but guide her wisely. Anne's warmth of feeling for the subject and for people, in almost equal measure, made her the ideal sounding-board. And it turned out just as she'd anticipated: Anne let her talk, then gently advised her as she saw fit, and our friend duly continued with her studies, graduating two years later.

Being taught by Anne was an adventure of discovery. Students in her groups were invited to see literature as language exquisitely at work, and to break down our literary prejudices against the science of linguistics so that we could find the tools with which to analyse the rhetoric of texts. Our own writing was also subjected to this kind of precise scrutiny by Anne, in ways that were not always comfortable but consistently enlightening. She had a firm sense of how poetry should work and what it should achieve, but at the same time allowed her students the freedom to follow their own paths and come to share her understanding in their own time. As another of our fellow students from Birmingham recalls, 'Anne let you work through your own vision; she didn't judge, or say that anything was indulgent or trivial'.

This friend remembers attending the Cambridge Poetry Festival of 1975 with her, and getting into a discussion on the journey home about whether it mattered if people could understand your poetry. 'One of the Cambridge Poets had said that it didn't matter if only three people understood a poem as long as it was good – by which I think the poet meant at the cutting edge of thought. On the other hand, Anne said that it did matter how many people read a poem, and whether they could understand it with simple concentration and fairly normal cultural knowledge, because in the end a poem is for communicating something important to other people, that enriches other lives. If a poem needs so much esoteric knowledge that only a handful of people understand it, then that chance is lost. It was not that she didn't value the clever poems written by the Cambridge Poets, but her instincts were always much more democratic, wanting to reach out and give poetry to as many people as possible.'

As a tutor, Anne went to great lengths to involve her creative writing students in the cultural life of the university as well as in the wider networks of contemporary poetry. She introduced them to the work of the Arvon Foundation, for which she was a regular tutor, and encouraged them to explore their writing in a variety of stimulating contexts. She herself drove that car-full of students to the Cambridge Poetry Festival (and back) and took pride in spurring them on to debate the social role of creative writing. At a later date she took a group of them to the funeral of another poet who had taught them, trusting that they would see themselves as witnesses to the importance of the writer's calling. It was also typical of Anne's kindness that she was concerned lest the turn-out at the funeral was poor and the young poet's already heartbroken family might suffer further distress.

In these actions, signs of the mature Anne known to us in the Vaughan Association were already shining through: a thoughtful respect for other people, intermingled with a passionate sense of the poet's vocation. Humanity and imagination, support and challenge, seriousness and a twinkle in the eye – these ingredients suggest the inspiring balancing-acts she undertook as a poet, and as a person.

For Anne, from Ann

ANN DRYSDALE

On the desk in front of me lies a small pile of postcards, each bearing the name of a beloved responsibility: sheep, horses, pigeons, hens, cats and various growing things, including a newly-planted chestnut tree. They are the instruction cards Anne Cluysenaar wrote out for me when I went to stay on the farm while she was in Belgium on family business, holding it for her, carrying out her rituals and making continuity in her image. I am still proud that she trusted me, and that I didn't let her down. When I heard about her death I took out these cards and dealt them, over and over, like a secret Tarot.

I met Anne first on a course at Tŷ Newydd that she tutored with Jeremy Hooker. It was called "the shape of your mind". I was a little overawed with the spiritual depth of the work of those two and remember being desperately hurt when Anne described me, in a one-to-one session, as "an occasional poet". I thought that meant the same sort of classification as a "Sunday painter" and I tried hard not to mind. I was so relieved when I found out the truth, and that is exactly what I am. We laughed about it later, when I met her again, teaching on my MA in Cardiff. I was able to pass on something new to Anne in due course.

When I began my course at Cardiff, I presented Anne with a short portfolio of my own poems and one in particular interested her. It was an occasional poem about an old Swaledale ram, a memory triggered by a poetry workshop with a different tutor. It was made out of the anger I'd felt when a skull was laid on the table and everybody went on about its spiritual dimensions and nobody seemed to see the intrinsic beauty of the thing, didn't appear to have any desire to know or understand sheep. I had spent twenty years running a smallholding in Yorkshire, very like what Anne had at Little Wentwood. I had won a first prize for sheep shearing.

I had thought twice before including that poem in the handful I gave her by way of introduction but although it drove a truck through her poetic principles, it was what established our common ground and began our friendship. It was what made her contact me, early in the relationship, when she wanted to spare her old Shetland Ram – her precious "Old Boy" – from the rough and tumble of the contract shearers. This was the verse that spoke to her:

> Somebody cared. He'd not have lived so long
> Without a good master. All of seven-shear.
> Keen, too. See in one horn the drilled hole
> Where they close-coupled him to a companion.
> Ramshackled, lest they tupped the ewes too soon.
> Seven times a fleece fell, damp and rank-smelling,
> Stained with the old musk, bedewed on the skin side
> With his essential oils. Oh, the rare stink of him
> In the height of the season.

Anne and I went out to the field at Little Wentwood and I sheared the Old Boy carefully by hand. Anne was keen to help and began lifting the wool up so I could cut it, but I explained to her that it was a shearer's rule never to do this. The wool should fall away from the shears under its own weight; to lift it up would make it more likely that I could cut the skin. It was probably the only thing I ever told Anne that she didn't already know.

So when we did a ritual exchange of recent books, playing the old game of signing them "Anne to Ann" and *vice versa*, and I read her poem "A Pekin Bantam", I was delighted to find a glancing reference to the need for that special kind of caution.

In the poem Anne tells of finding a hen frozen in a tray of ice, and cutting it free with scissors. She sees the problem: 'to sever not flesh and bone / (her breast in my left hand), only icicles, quills'. I was taken back over the years to the evening in the field when I kicked the first half of the fleece aside and rolled the Old Boy over to relieve him of the rest of it, showing off my own pennyworth of expertise.

When I first read that poem it made me want to laugh. But now, when I read it and remember, it makes me want to cry.

December 11

A Pekin bantam

I have had to rescue a hen from a trayful of ice.
She must have slept there too long. It melted. It froze.
In the morning, her legs were held fast by their long feathers,
her body silent and still but for its eye.

I couldn't understand at first and tried to lift her.
Had to put her down again while I fetched the scissors.
Then, the problem. To sever not flesh and bone
(her breast in my left hand), only icicles, quills.

When she hobbled, joining the others, I thought: 'Have I cut
a claw after all?' No. That leg was just iced
to a wing. Snip. Now the tray of still-frozen water
remains in the yard, marked by a ring of feathers.

Soon where she sat is iced over again, but the warmth
that leaked has left a trace fossil, darker and clearer,
as if, in the past of her almost-death, she has left
what matters only to us, who show it each other.

(Anne Cluysenaar, *Touching Distances*, p.13)]

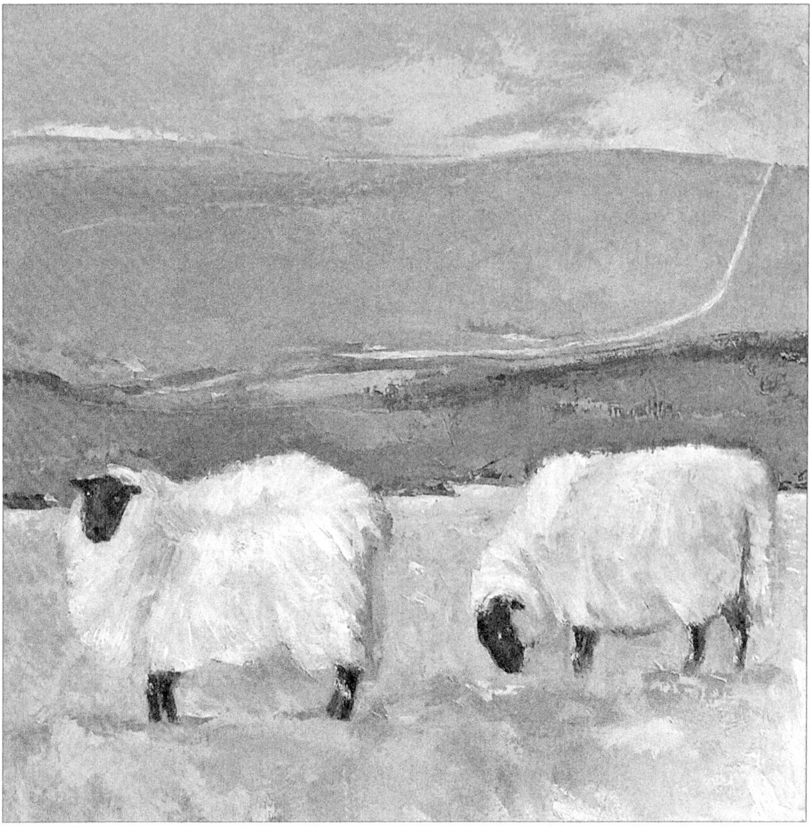

PAUL MATTHEWS

Far Off

At the top of the field was a bench.
I sat on it in the sun and gazed
a long way to where grass meets sky.

I was sad at how far off things were
and asked what most do I want
and I said for this ache in my chest

to be bound with a skein of blue.
Distance was endless. Nothing nearby
that I looked at had a *You* inside it.

Gathering Nectar

When somebody gets buried
(my granddaughter asks)
does their 'syrup' go with them?

And I say *surely not*; surely
a sweet air hums in the grass
over their requiem.

•

All flesh is grass.
This flowering

meadow (mowed
and mowed again)

returns abundantly.
Sweet clover, testify.

What other evidence
than love is needed.

Writing among Animals

Here we are, plus one horse. Time slows.
I'm glad the far ring of hills is holding us.

•

Clouds shape thoughts for this breath only.
Cows turn to graze on our strange behaviour.

•

How could our words come close enough
to sound what wells in their kind eyes?

•

They don't mind us. Their gut makes milk
of any news they get from a green page.

•

Sheep far off cry their lives. We strangers
share the field with them. I love this place.

Look up the root of the word 'nectar' and you will find that 'nec', as in 'necropolis', means 'death' and that 'tar' is the 'overcoming' of it.

SEÁN STREET

Fieldfares

Anne Cluysenaar, November, 2014

It's a misnomer when we call them small hours,
an interminable place to live, bringing back
the sleepless absolute of things we'll never mend.
Nothing for it, just listen to north-easterlies'
all-night storm broadcasts transmitted from the Baltic.

But to see through eventual dawn those sudden
birds' dissolve across the garden – the morning's gift of it –
is to encounter a definition of you
in what we might have shared: 'Look, Fieldfares, we've Fieldfares!'
as they shoal round, leafing winter trees' antennae.

They've flown towards us for millennia of miles,
even after that profligate in their circling,
exhausting our space, one wing for all, filling air
harbours with verticity while somewhere emptied
past summers echo their departure's bereavement.

There are things, Keats wrote to Bailey, require greetings
of the spirit to give them existence, fleeting
engagements in thin places, advent transmissions,
consecrations in skies, clouds. And understanding
this migrant flight, searching the winds for a presence.

RIC HOOL

Incantation

when walls are see through protection
when art misses the mark
when wine is watered down
the country mouse flees town
                              stay close

stay close   brick on brick tock to tick

when rivers ice when roads skid
when clocks stop   pens dry
and glue becomes unstuck

when sky is rent   tumblers
taken flight   when night finds day
and leaves shaken away
when crumpled paper is cast to bin
words become mutterings   when meaning slips
its rightful place – Muse fallen from grace
                              stay close

till Y returns to twig   O to acorn cup
and Q once more indwells its shell
stay close
        warp to weft   tree to bark
              root to earth   zag to zig

MYRA SCHNEIDER

His gift from Brazil

is enclosed in a wooden box that's weighty and inviting
as Pandora's. I can't wait to prise open its neatly planed lid.

Inside, dark as the deepest amber masking the death-sprawl
of the insect it trapped millennia ago when it was a pool of resin,

is a superior preserve which would frown at jam trickling
down the side of its container. Like the opinionated, it refuses

to budge but I manage to dig out a spoonful and spread it thickly
over melting butter on the pocked surface of a crumpet.

The first bite is into the softest cushion of utter sweetness.
It tastes of petals flaring on flame trees, paradise flowers,

parrot plumage, the green ferment of foliage and frond,
of shade pulsing with insects and hidden spirits yet it's mellow

as English sunlight in late September, as the first yellowing
of long-fingered leaves on the sycamores beyond my garden.

The second bite tastes of unstoppable abundance, sends me
out to the sunflowers, giants who sprang up in summer, ghosts now.

Their huge heads gripped by green claws dwarf my hand's span.
They're brittle – a piece breaks off from one. It's bristly as a broom

but it houses so many nutritious seeds in its cells I could harvest
these ghosts, plant the needy world with chrome and ochre glory.

The last bite tastes of healing. I dream this delicacy is quietening
my mind, easing stubborn joints, enriching blood as it flows

round my body, feeding overdry skin like rain moistening
starved ground. Suddenly I see those halleluiahs of luminous gold

which stream from sun and horizon in a late Turner watercolour
where sea and sky are inseparable. Gently, I close the wooden box.

The First of Spring

for Anne Cluysenaar

A honey sun, the cease of gnawing wind
so we seize the day, unleash ourselves
in the country park, gaze at flowers inscribed *To Dad*

lying on a bench. They summon a huge bee
to their pink and yellow freesia bells. Dreamily,
I too enter the nectar-laden chambers and feed.

Turning away, we follow *the droghte of March* track
to the water garden where snowdrops are fading,
daffodils are on the brink of opening

and expectation's in bloom on naked trees.
Welters of lily stalks in the darks of a pond
are tangles of umbilical cords. Beyond the garden,

beyond the singing of birds is a lake which glitters
as if it's a source of light. We sit down
on a wicker seat and there you are breathing

in the budding warmth, freed from the last
of October now and that distressed message
you sent before your life was snatched.

You're stooping over a small plant, stroking
its leaves, tracking the hover-rise of a damsel-fly,
smiling as you follow all the riverlets.

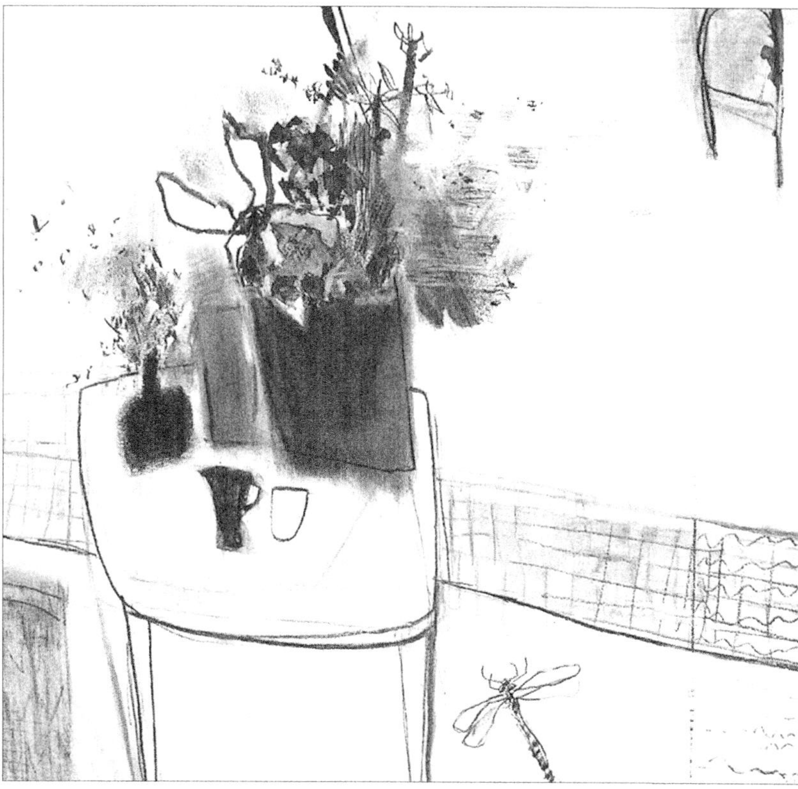

Reflections on Anne Cluysenaar at Lancaster and in Wales

CHARLES WILKINSON

Nodes (The Dolmen Press, Poetry Ireland Editions, 1970)
Touching the Distances (Cinnamon Press, 2014)

In the late sixties and early seventies, members of Lancaster University's Poetry Society met in the upstairs room of the Shakespeare. Poets and audience sprawled on the floor or leant against the walls; possibly the provision of seating would have been regarded as a bourgeois affectation. Only two members of the university's English department were regularly present: David Craig, the Marxist critic and editor of the Penguin *Selected Poems of Hugh MacDiarmid*, and Anne Cluysenaar, who taught General Linguistics as well as English Literature. They were the two members of faculty to whom young poets would show their work, both generous with their time and unfailingly courteous to students. Anne was also the founder of *Continuum*, the university's literary magazine. She was highly regarded by the student editorial board, whose efforts she oversaw.

At that time the student taste was for the Liverpool poets and Adrian Mitchell; the predominant tone political or subversively surrealistic: earnest, angry poems about Vietnam leavened with imitations of Spike Hawkins and Pete Brown. In contrast, Anne's poems were formally exact, learned, suffused with the imagery of light and water:

> Foliage echoes in its arches the blunt
> Explosions of light behind it in brightening
> Sequence, silhouetted, translucent, shining,
>
> Descending to a sea which suspends the beat
> Like the first sun after snowfall
> Or the first touch of potential lovers.
> ('Shadows')

Writing against the prevailing ethos, her references were to classical mythology rather than Che Guevera. Yet she was always given a respectful hearing. Possibly we sensed that, whilst her style was not fashionably *engagè*, her work would prove more durable than the agit-prop then current. When her collection *Nodes* appeared in 1970, many of us bought it. The poem 'Orpheus', the final quatrain of which is used to dedicate the book to the memory of her mother, Sybil Fitzgerald Cluysenaar, is perhaps indicative of her distance from the zeitgeist of those days:

> Though she is dead, she was,
> And became herself through time.
> Her memory lives in life-praise
> And at the point of creation.

As a regular reviewer, Anne was informed about the poets then writing, but she eschewed the merely fashionable; sometimes her predilection was for the overlooked and almost forgotten. I remember her speaking enthusiastically about the work of Burns Singer, who died in his thirties. Anne subsequently edited his *Selected Poems* in 1977. Although Singer's poems were later thought sufficiently strong to merit a collected edition from Carcanet, it is perhaps fair to say he remains a marginal figure.

Lancaster at that time was a turbulent institution, troubled by sit-ins and demonstrations similar to those that had started at the Sorbonne in 1968 and then crossed the Channel to the LSE and Essex. Although far from being a card-carrying communist, Anne was not politically neutral; she was definitely of the left. When David Craig's argument with the Head of the English Department led to his dismissal, Anne was one of those who supported him until he was re-employed by the University. He later established Creative Writing as a separate department at Lancaster.

Like many former students at Lancaster, I owe Anne a great debt. I first met her when I was eighteen. She read my poems and provided hospitality and helpful criticism at her home in Lancaster. When she was teaching at Birmingham University, she looked at my manuscript and invited me to the English Department to discuss my work. All this was especially generous as I had never been her pupil. Students of hers at Lancaster included David Ward, a poet and editor of the little magazine *Smoke*; the novelist and poet, Nigel Grey; the speculative fiction writers D.F. Lewis and P.F. Jeffery and Robert Fisk, *The Independent's* Middle East correspondent.

I lost touch with Anne when she left Birmingham to take up a post in Yorkshire, but I continued to read her perceptive reviews in *Stand*, which were informed by her professional expertise in Stylistics; for many years, she was one of that long standing journal's leading poetry critics and usually reviewed in tandem with Terry Eagleton.

Although I knew Anne had moved to Wales and was editing *Scintilla*, I did not meet her again until I started attending the readings at the Hen and Chickens in Abergavenny. I found her every bit as kindly, humorous and perceptive as when I had known her at Lancaster. Having lost contact with my university contemporaries, it was a joy to have someone with whom I could exchange memories of those times. She amused me by recalling how the poet Nigel Grey, the most prominent anarchist on campus, whose removal skills she'd unaccountably preferred to Pickford's, accidentally broke her nose whilst helping her to transport furniture to her new home.

As Ric Hool and Anne had books out from Cinnamon Press, Colin Sutherill and I asked them to read at a Red Parrot poetry event in Presteigne. On that occasion, Anne read extracts from her diary poems *Touching Distances*. The contrast and continuities with her earlier work in *Nodes* suggest what makes Anne's work as a poet distinctive. As befits the nature of the project in her later book, the tone is more conversational; the quotidian is privileged in a way that is sometimes absent from her earlier poems. Although now co-existing with the everyday, her metaphysical caste of mind is still evident: Anne developed the unusual knack of marrying the numinous to the empirical. As always her clarity of diction and scrupulous sonorities show a refined ear for language matched by her mastery of form.

Whilst Anne is very much a poet of the particular, noticing the minutiae that would pass unremarked by a less observant witness – the subtle shifting of light in a valley, a wasps' nest, petals, a hoof print – she is much more than a painterly writer providing accurate verbal landscapes but little more; in her work, there is often something half-glimpsed, a fleeting movement in the corner of the eye, or even a sense of the 'not quite visible', the imperceptible ripples of the eternal in the phenomenal world.

Touching Distances is in part a record of a life lived at the edge of the Wentworth Forest on the Welsh Marches; however, it transcends the pastoral in its engagement with the wider culture of her times. Poems on the Kepler telescope and the Higgs boson show Anne was not only knowledgeable about the scientific discoveries of the past but also alert to contemporary advances. She remains in dialogue with her predecessors. April 9th is a poem written 'At the Grave of Henry Vaughan,' which reminds us of the stripe of metaphysical verse that Anne found of more than historical value; she shared that poet's preoccupation with 'light', which becomes in her work more than a motif: perhaps almost a mode of perception that places her within the wider illuminationist tradition.

I still had my copy of *Nodes*, and at sixty-three I was able to ask Anne to sign a work purchased for ten shillings at the age of nineteen. Turning to the fly-leaf, I see that Anne has written: 'Bought in The Shakespeare, Lancaster, 1970 – signed during a Red Parrot reading, May 2014 – A reading for *Touching Distances* indeed!'

I last saw Anne in the Angel Hotel, Abergavenny in September 2014. I'd arranged to meet friends from Ystragynlais. Anne came in afterwards and though she greeted me warmly she declined to join us. She had some papers with her and was plainly looking forward to a quiet hour on the conspicuously comfortable sofa she'd commandeered. She waved when I got up to leave. We agreed we would inevitably run into each other at the Hen and Chicks. That was not to be. In November Ric Hool emailed with the news of her tragic death.

Although *Touching Distances* dips less frequently into the myth kitty than *Nodes*, Anne returns to the legend of Orpheus in her poem of January 27:

> It's the head that stays with me, severed, afloat,
> but singing still on its way to the sea . . .

lines that tell us that the poet and musician Orpheus's work are separate from his life and will survive his violent death. Anne has bequeathed us a considerable body of poetry and critical writing and editing, all of which will repay continued study and will be returned to by discerning readers of poetry, both outside and within the academe, as well as being cherished by those who knew her. If her lyre, unlike Orpheus's, will not hang amongst the stars, we can at least be thankful she has left what will surely prove to be a lasting legacy.

An edited version of these reflections was read by at the author at an event on April 1 2015 in The Hen and Chickens, Abergavenny, where poets and friends gathered to celebrate her life and work.

MARY MACGREGOR

Siluria siluriensis

I walked to the quarry
but a stone's throw from where I live.
I leaned on a gate.
In scooped out rock were two platforms
grassed and grazed by sheep
that for a moment
stopped their grazing to look at me.
Surrounding the two platforms
shale on end rose up.
And Anne, I thought of you.

I knew this quarry was special.
This shale held the secrets of time.
Here they found the first signs of life on land,
the first cells bubbling and doubling
into moss-like vascular plants.
Here, a flick in time,
a mere four hundred million years ago,
a signature of the Silurian series.
And you, Anne, had learned to read it.

How I regret I shall never bring you here.
For me, this quarry now belongs to you
and you to it. You are Queen of the Quarry.
Without your ever having known it,
this quarry is inscribed in your poetry
and your poetry in the quarry.
Together they proclaim
the interconnectedness of all things.

What's more on the strata of your past,
you came to live in the land of the Silures-
the last stratum of your life.
Anne – Siluria Siluriensis.

NORMAN SCHWENK

Quintet for Anne

Funny how you seemed
to fit in with a bunch of
literary guys

without becoming
a substitute man – never
less of a woman.

We were a little
in awe of you, I believe:
you stuck to your guns

yet had a gentle
touch – no energy wasted
on ego trips or

hasty conclusions;
there was always time for your
rich rolling chuckle.

DAVID HART

I imagined

I imagined you were walking behind me
as I walked my poem
but when I looked around
there were many of you walking
blurred together and
out of step
all in the same clothes
each looking with the same eyes
and I saw a collision of worlds,
of words, of worlds, of
present and absent, of absent and
present, each with a shaky, a border
mindful of a whole life at the
spinning gate, then again
looked back and this time
there was one of you, smiling,
in that moment only I caught it,
so I tip-toed on, eyes closed, because
I was here still and unstill, sightful
and blind, whole
and fractured, and would like this poem
for a second
to live
along the track now.

February 2015

NEIL CURRY

The Well

Though he leant right out over the rim,
The water was too far down for him to see.

"Time, you realise," someone remarked
Inside his head, "is only the rate

At which the past decays." And so,
He let slip slowly through his fingers,

The one or two choice memories he chanced
To have about him, then stood listening

Attentively for their depleted echo.

HELEN MOORE

Deep Time, Deep Tissue

For L

Here on the altar to multi-dimensional experience
I'm prostrate and naked (from the waist veiled
with a towel), face ensconced in a leatherette crescent
through which I may disappear

        Your fingers beginning cool, now radiate the Sun
        into layers of dermis, subcutaneous fat
        towards the deeper muscle, at first following the grain
        working with awareness, a mental

        Gray's Anatomy (all red-raw & flayed!) and your honed
        sense of intuition. Slowly, where your deft hands
        press, my body's armour is assuaged – those knots
        tight as rivets, these flat metallic plates

        tensioned as if to snap, these blades tempered
        bands of steel. Time expanding and warmth in oily kneading
        start to release the stress and toxins, which life
        in the Anthropocene engenders in our being

        *

Much later I'll sob like a child
a stream of dammed emotion gushing out
which left me feeling lighter, as if
I really had shouldered a burden

        but for now I float – am foetus
        deep sea mammal
        first bubble of life
        in some primordial lagoon

This aching body that at times
I've hated, softens as its contours roll
this body formed from dust of stars

(ah, the energy rippling through us now!)

Deep time, deep tissue —
eyes form black holes. Sometimes I'm dark matter
drawing everything towards me, swallowing it in
(the way Nut swallows the Sun)
making follicles, cells, poems

This 'me' rapidly collapsing, this 'me'
a mere speck, a gleam in Time's eye
yet developed and refined
over millions of years
in our symbiotic home

*

Earth, this home that awed
our brave-new astronauts —

wild, animate planet
set in cosmic velvet —

inestimable worth, curves
drifting blue and white

*

O, Anthropocene
period of consequences!

In a pinch of geological time our minds
have made deserts of grasslands

dead-zones in oceans, have cut away
vast sections of rainforest 'lung'

erasing cultures of birds, animals, people
eroding soils elaborated for millennia

    We knowing humans
    disrupting the grand cycles

        of biology, chemistry, geology, knowingly persist
        in filling the atmosphere with gases

            which trap the Sun's rays
            melting glaciers, turning seas acidic

        and where our ice-sheets melt
        prospect for yet more of Gaia's bitter blood.

O, obscene era
this is an emergency!

        *

We breathe, releasing the enormity
of this awareness. How I love

        and thank you, dearest Body! You
        ancient, four-zoaed temple

open to the skies and aligned to Polaris –
hub around which all other stars

        wheel. In whatever mortal span
        that remains, help me to navigate

this crisis in our evolution, to stay
with what others have begun

        millions of cells rising
        in and for our life-source, Earth

    willing Ecozoa's birth

Note:

The current geological epoch, named the Holocene, encompasses the growth and impacts of industrial civilisation on our planetary ecosystems. Given these impacts, which have global significance for the future evolution of all living species, a new term 'Anthropocene' was proposed in 2000 by Paul Crutzen & Eugene Stoermer to denote the present time interval. However, critics say that this overstates and reinforces a human-centred perspective, and deprives us of an inspiring vision for a new ecological age. My neologism 'Ecozoa' encapsulate this, and references Blake's 'Four Zoas'.

Sequences in the Poetry of Anne Cluysenaar

JOHN KILLICK

Looking at the range of Anne's work it becomes clear that sequences played a major part in it. Addressing themes sequentially was obviously the way her mind and imagination worked: she doesn't make definitive statements but a series of forays into a territory, gradually building up a whole which is often more than the sum of its parts. For example, each of the twenty-three 'Vaughan Variations' (probably her finest achievement) accommodates various themes and approaches within its span, but we take away from it an overall impression to which all of these diversions have contributed. One gets the impression that Anne worked slowly and published sparingly. Although she was clearly an intellectual, and her work is redolent of wide reading and deep thought, she almost always starts from, and returns to, ordinary experiences and discrete sense-impressions to ground her meditations.

There are eleven sequences in her work. The first four ('On the Skyline', 'Poems of Memory', 'Open Ways' and 'Timeslips') have much in common. Three of these first appeared in her first book *Double Helix* and were reprinted in her second *Timeslips*. The fourth was new in that volume. Time, memory and the changing rural scene are shared by all of them, though each has its particular emphasis. The starting-point may be a creature, a fossil, a landscape, a season, a person, a photograph, a relationship, a domestic task. They often widen out to encompass description, memory, philosophical reflection. There is a sense of the teasing out of insights in a calm, unhurried way, and yet there is also an intensity, even urgency, about the process. Anne was always on the look-out for parallels, continuities, for making sense of history in a personal and global context, but she was honest enough to acknowledge dissimilarities and incongruities on the way. The reader shares her excitement through being included in the search, but the journey to enlightenment never becomes frenetic or incoherent because the poems are the refining of that process.

'Letters and Memoirs' is from the earliest of these sequences. It begins with a photograph of Anne's grandmother holding her mother as a child in her arms.

This is a poignant evocation of a relationship that was to falter, yet at the time was clearly most meaningful:

> this true image
> of a bond neither could afterwards recall.

We learn of the emotion which is expressed in the pose of:

> grandmother's smile, the shining lower lip,
> soft, surely loving, the large capable hand
> on which my mother's fist, clenched in delight
> has left a tender shadow.

We are then told of the letters and memoirs written by the grandmother from India, of the breakdown she suffered, and of the separation from her child. Anne then compares this picture with another, this time of her mother holding her forty-two years later, and how it mirrors the stance in the earlier photograph of 1894. She invokes a geological image to give a further time perspective to the scene:

> the fragile shapes of our ancestors flow still
> on the drift of a tide turned these three million years.
> They settled, just so, one day, one forgotten moment.

There follows a reference to the Christmas just passed in which Anne notes that no Mother and Child cards have been received. We are told that it is snowing heavily outside. The poem ends with the lines:

> The typewriter drops its silt into the silence.
> Those hours, and these, in all their details of writing,
> of reading, are now invisible fossils that no one
> could recall. All the prints are laid down together.

There are so many reverberations in these lines. The 'silt' suggests not just the snow but the sand in the hourglass. The 'writing' can be that of the fossil in the rock, the letters and diaries, and the poem itself. The 'prints' again can have triple meanings: the fossil again, the photographs, and the words coming out of the poet's printer. The poem is only forty-three lines long, but it gathers in so much in its short span.

'Vaughan Variations', which is the culmination of the *Timeslips* volume, is similarly wide-ranging in its reflective scope, but here there is the added level of reference to the great Welsh metaphysical. Each poem carries a quote from Vaughan's writing at its head, and some of them refer to his preoccupations or evoke incidents in his biography. Each poem adopts a different viewpoint and is written in a different form. In this work Anne pushed herself further than elsewhere, and the result is a virtuosic masterpiece that should be much better known. Some of the finest variations do not refer to Vaughan directly. Number fifteen, for example, is a description of the dawn, and here Anne attains a stylistic fluidity not previously found in her work:

> I look up and the stars too
> are almost gone. The Plough
> plunges blade first out of sight,
> only its handle still bright and high.
> Now with the naked eye
> I can see the spin, how shadow
> filters to blue
> over green, and the sky, come nearer, begins to
> mottle with blobs and rifts of dark and light.

Amongst contemporaries only Mimi Khalvati in her *Entries on Light* book sequence has attained a comparable tranced lyricism.

Number sixteen carries the subtitle 'On the sudden death of a friend's wife' so one is astonished to find that it does not address that subject directly but reflects:

> being astonished that
> the world was still there
> and myself still seeing it.

The rest of the poem consists of a description of glimpsing a doe in a field fleetingly, and unsuccessfully attempting a further encounter:

> I found it hard to imagine
> the weight of the doe, so flat
> and white she looked, stepping
> in profile behind the may,
> her neck vertical as a periscope.
> Any warmth she had breathed
> into this air, invisible now,
> must be drifting with the pale seeds

of the sallow in a great bank
of slow-moving forest breath.

The utter simplicity of this writing is astonishing, as if the poet has cast aside all artifice in favour of truth-telling in its essence.

Anne's next sequence is the book-length *Batu-Angas: Envisioning Nature with Alfred Russel Wallace*. Her subject was co-discoverer with Darwin of the theory of natural selection, explored the Malay archipelago, and found many new or rare species, including the magnificent butterfly *Ornithoptera Croesus Croesus*. She explains her title as follows:

> It derives from the poem about Ternate where it is explained that 'batu-angas' means 'burnt rock' or cooled lava. The emphasis on a molten core on which the tectonic plates move is appropriate, I think, to the remarkable insights Wallace had concerning biogeography and the origin of the species – his emphasis on the interaction of geological time and massive or relatively small terrestrial transformations within biological change.

So the poem emerges from considerable research, and marks an escalation in Anne's interest in scientific processes. Throughout the sequence she displays a remarkable command of complex subject-matter. In some ways the poem resembles 'Vaughan Variations'. There are twenty-two parts, and each one is prefaced by a quote from Wallace. But it is much more focused on its inspirer, and many sections also contain quotations from Wallace's works (rather like MacDiarmid does in his 'In Memoriam James Joyce', though he did not always acknowledge his sources!). The determination to follow the Wallace trail has something dogged about it, and the decision to incorporate the Wallace prose style inevitably causes the sequence to drag in places, but there are some wonderful passages, and some very fine individual poems.

The opening poem is one of the latter. It is about the butterfly *Croesus*. Anne goes to see it in the Natural History Museum. The excitement of this visit is well conveyed, and the ending, with its characteristic time reference, is beautifully articulated:

> As I catch a trace
>   of Wallace's fine-tipped quill
>   on the tiny round of the lapel

> and the dull glint of the pin
> through that wizened thorax,
> I think of a mind's movement
> stilled between pages,
> as dead, as rich –
>
> ready in another mind
> to fly, and settle.

This certainly whets the appetite to embark upon Anne's longest and most ambitious sequence.

Anne's last three collections mark two developments in her work: a greater productivity (a pamphlet and two books in seven years), and a gradual loosening of style. Nothing of the same complexity was attempted, and the sequences generally are more diverse without losing coherence. I propose to discuss the collection *Migrations* first, because of the links of *Water to Breathe* (which came out first) with *Touching Distance*, which came last. *Migrations* contains three very different sequences. The book opens with 'On the Farm'; these are vivid descriptions of rural life. They lack an overall theme but present an integrated portrait of the sights and sounds and processes of the agricultural environment. They are very straightforward, and presage the journal approach Anne was working towards.

'Through Time' is very different, probably Anne's best and most profound short sequence. It consists of fifteen brief meditations inspired by landscapes and concentrating on their geological underpinnings. They display considerable knowledge of tectonic and erosional processes and make a series of points about the span of a human life in contrast to that of the earth. They show an astonishing clarity of thought and expression, as evinced by this extract from 'Up Gwrellech Stream':

> Together we walk on.
> Over seas that are now rock.
> Over mountains that were once desert.
> Over sands that rivers washed down
> from distant peaks
> to make a now vanished shore.
> It seems that 'now',
> the word itself, becomes more and more
> strange to us with every step up the stream.

One of the most legitimate demands we may make of artists in any medium is to provide us with insights into some of the most fundamental aspects of life on earth; things which we otherwise might miss, but which have profound implications for our understanding of our place in the scheme of things. Norman Nicholson does it memorably in some of his geological poems: 'The Motion of the Earth', for example, where we learn that we go:

> Seeking the seeming familiar, though every stride
> Takes us a thousand miles from where we were before.

And MacDiarmid in his 'On a Raised Beach':

> The moon moves the waters backwards and forwards,
> But the stones cannot be lured an inch farther
> Either on this side of eternity or the other.

With 'Through Time' Anne triumphantly joins their company.

The title sequence consists of twenty-four short lyrics of a fairly disparate nature, which are like diary entries, but not labelled as such. They share an approach with all of the pamphlet *Water to Breathe*; indeed some texts are the same. The pamphlet, however, is bound together by a common theme – that of childhood. They are not conventional reminiscences, but snapshots of all kinds of events, some ecstatic, some poignant, some mysterious. There is also a prose piece providing background, so that unlike the poems of the *Migrations* or *Touching Distances* sequences, we are provided with a context in which to set them. Some of this is personal writing of a high order. For example, in the poem beginning 'Seeing that woman walk across a field' (none of them have titles) two experiences are telescoped: the present moment and its counterpart in the past. The distinction between them is blurred, so that we are presented with a highly charged situation in all its complexity. We are convinced of the authenticity of an event which remains inexplicable.

Touching Distances: Diary Poems is the furthest Anne has gone in her published work in embracing the intimate and exploiting the immediate. There are seventy-five poems encompassing two years. They retain a certain casual quality, with the language more informal than elsewhere. This is from 'January 13: 'Hunting the Higgs', written some months before the momentous discovery was made:

> No wonder they love a laugh, the physicists,
> What ever they find or don't, it's ok.

> Symmetries of the world just remnants
> of those which, if perfect, would only have led to
>
> no world at all – anti-matter, matter
> would have cancelled each other out. Maybe.
> Or maybe not, if the theory is at fault.
> And if it is? More exciting still.

Here the inner and outer questioning characteristic of the poet is given a new urgency by the almost chattiness of its embodiment, showing that right to the end the poet was pushing at the boundaries of ideas and their presentation.

Anne was undoubtedly on a journey, and, had she lived longer, was unlikely ever to have reached a destination which fully satisfied her. All of her poems display homogeneity and diversity, intellectual probing and subtle sensitivity, and the sequence provided the flexible format to best suit her needs.

This essay is a revised and extended version of one published in Quattrocento 3 *(2006).*

JEREMY HILTON

from a Derbyshire sequence

1.

the thraldom of history
    marks these lands
lines on the valley sides
    or broken walls
ruined houses hidden in trees
    roofs half missing

in the wooded slope the surprise
    of the great cleft
clammed from the harshness of
    sunlight and law
man's dark age oppression
    in the name of God

to the west green farmland
    reaches to Wales
to the north the moors rise
    high and browner
to the east hidden valleys and green
hills with strange-shaped peaks

many dales are dry, some stony
    rough on the ankles
    redstart country
others grassy and open
    reaching to the sky

but then the rivers
    only the rivers
rivers fast-running over rocks
rivers of crystal water
    purer than paradise

    rivers where dippers delight
        to feed and breed

    rivers with far to go
no premonition of salt seas
where waters will lose themselves at last
after many turns of the
        compass, confluences
rivers a heaven within a heaven hidden

*(the great cleft is known as Lud's Church, a
meeting-place for Lollards and other persecuted
puritan sects of the late Middle-Ages / early
Renaissance period, also associated with The
Green Knight of earlier legend)*

2. (i.m. Anne Cluysenaar)

there is a heart to this landscape of hills
and sounding streams that fall like precious rain
with borders of broken stone and
distances measured in one world or the next

so the shout goes out
        echoing valley walls
and vast wildernesses newly explored
for a soul that now dwells
        around these hills
and words heard over wider worlds
        soaring on four wild winds

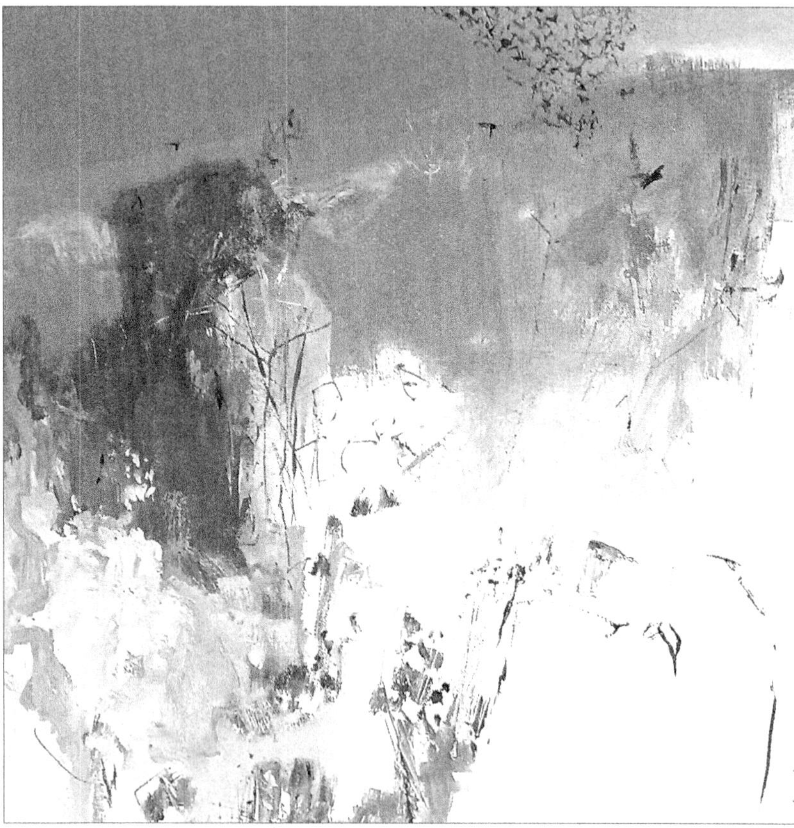

COLIN MOSS

The Sheaves of Day

"Man cannot afford . . . to look at Nature directly . . .
He must look through and beyond her"
– Thoreau's Journal, 23 March 1853

1 – August

Stubble scrapes against shoes, on the field edge;
but the rising slope of the Down, moulded and animate, lies still –
sleeping and not sleeping;
while the whole life-force of grass and trees,
the sky's fire-clouds and coloured dusk,
breathes the will of living things,
the dreams of rocks,
and the daily transpiration
of the wild, untameable levity.

Something is thrusting into time
in this dry valley, littered with sheep dung,
running with unanswerable questions –
the future of this stone, of the hand that holds it,
and the past life that made it;

and we have to partake,
– to see beyond this flint's stony face,
find what only minds can give, and purvey;
and somehow love it, this path up to the dragon ridge,
these disparate sights, the closing of seasons,
the life and half-life,
in these fields of riddles, waiting for harvest.

2 – September

A blaze of sky above,
beneath, warm green of the down,
and nests in straw;
a whole amphitheatre of land, and the sounds of sheep –
the trees, grass, birds,
resting in the still –

something is happening
as the dusk approaches, something like a lying down in small hollows,
and the leaves preparing for sleep;

if it were possible
to learn just one word of what this is,
    the mystery of day slowly becoming night,
    it would transform us –
to know
    what the sun leaves behind as it sets,
    what sustains us until the dawn –
the syllables surround us, but the words are
a language of the wind,
that tonight is silent;

life here is the sights and sounds of the chalkland,
what we see;
how we choose to see;

and if one of us, by the field gate,
quietly, watching –
    thankful –
    could whisper that one word,
would only the dawn
understand?

3 – October

The moon creeps behind the thorn branch
across the sky
– but does not move;
it is us – the field gate, the tree,
and the earth, that turn, ever-pacing the perimeter, seeking new stars,
waking to new mornings, a measured tread,
wiser than clocks,
circling through this cloud of unknowing,
spinning with this invisible shield of air.

To stop at the end of the day
is to see, not rest,
but that everything below us is in motion,
that we are the slingshot of the sun;

and know that ever carried over the ring of the sea
is a swell of surf that spreads
from beaches to continents, egged on by the moon,
who lags behind the day
to watch and follow, long after
we have bid the sun a dusk's farewell.

This journey of evening, the end and the beginning
the same movement; we die – others live;
the trees will wait for the light, as the evening gathers up in its sheets
the conversations of the day, for remembrance – the words, spoken slowly,
meld into soft leather, and slip across the landscape,
settling into the hollows of the hill,
lying peacefully on the lynchets, content to wait for the call.

The moon chuckles and carries on;
the hills wait for us to catch up;
there is a pattern, and we tread the day into its moulds,
releasing, perhaps, from its fading scent,
a whisper, more ancient than tides,
into the flowing of air through our voices,
that frost into the breath of the turning world,
to carry its cargo through the night.

4 – The last dusk

But life is movement; a day
chasing itself across the ever-breathing sky,
the wrestling of sense and desire
making a fresh time-stamp on the page of flesh,
an hour shored against the unknown,

so that memory's wharf will, that last day, provide our crossing point
to skirt the estuary sands
where the new ferryman waits, oars ready,
with a welcoming smile, "It is only the world going round", he says,
"only another day on your journey".

Trailing our hands in the water,
we sip that final reminder – death is movement,
a step of life,
in which Sun and Moon continue to carry souls,
looking upon every last minute of joy and anguish,
every last morning;

do not think then of permanence;
think only of the new songs to be learned
and the remembered syllables of solitary evenings
beneath the travelling moon, following the sunset,
in that valley where the ages speak of winters' harvests
sown in you,

to be threshed, and sown again
in the fields of time, that are in your care.

Anne Cluysenaar

ROGER HUBANK

I first met Anne in 1997 at the second Colloquium of the Usk Valley Vaughan Association, as it was known then. My cousin, the poet Mercer Simpson, asked me to go with him, and I was sufficiently curious to accept his invitation, though at that time I had no particular interest in Henry Vaughan, and knew as much about his work as one might expect of an academic whose primary interests lay outside the 17th century.

The Colloquium was held that year at Penpont, perhaps the most agreeable of our various venues, a 17th century house beside the Usk a few miles west of Brecon. It was, I remember, a particularly cold weekend, and the house itself – it had no central heating – was bitterly cold. A night-crossing of the Arctic wastes of that enormous landing in search of a loo was a daunting prospect. If the house as a whole was cold, not so our talks and discussions. They were conducted before a great fire burning in a fireplace of baronial proportions, in a drawing-room furnished with deep, comfortable armchairs and what can only be described, in such a superior setting, as 'sofas' (not 'settees').

Wynn Thomas was there, and Donald Allchin, and Jonathan Nauman as well as other now familiar figures who were to become friends in years to come. Bob Wilcher spoke about 'Henry Vaughan and the Church', and Jerry Hooker, sunk deep in one of those great armchairs beside the fire, gave his talk on 'Quickness'; Peter Thomas, too, talking Wordsworth with me in front of the dying embers long after everyone else had gone to bed. And of course Anne. Anne welcomed everyone. She would have been, as Yeats put it, 'your heartiest welcomer'.

That same year she published *Timeslips* containing her 'Vaughan Variations', which became for me – she later presented me with a copy – my first real introduction, albeit an indirect one, to Henry Vaughan. One poem, the fifth Variation with its stark headnote 'Dead I was and deep in trouble', spoke to me with especial force.

After months in the this and that,
hardly trying to live as joy

can let you, I'm grit dry.
Through love, was his way. To a sense
of God. Attention becoming prayer.

If she had known the arid consequences, that dullness of spirit of the creative life gone dead – well, so had I. The deadness of 'the this and that'. And so a sense of kinship was born, and a sense, too, that Henry Vaughan might have something to say to me.

'Attention' was also Anne's way. 'Hold fast,' says Denise Levertov, a poet she greatly admired, 'to what seems ephemera . . . Nothing much, or everything; all depends / on how you regard it.' And so she did. A short poem, 'Together', published in *Scintilla 7*, in doing precisely that, raises a question about the nature of identity, about what it is we belong to, as if our real being is somehow beyond the self.

> There were dark leaves spread out
> so that the air between shone
> as it narrowed, stretched, shivered.
>
> A bird, never catching its breath,
> sang invisibly, not hidden
> yet not seen by me,
>
> and from the gravel by my foot
> a darker-than-red, a crimson
> poppy swayed on a thin stalk.
>
> It seemed we were all – tree
> and air and bird and poppy and
> gravel even – composing together
>
> a secret no one of us
> could know, not one escape.
> Which breathes itself in us.

Note the shift in the last line. The poet, no longer an autonomous agent, separated from an external world which she observes, has been absorbed within a single unity, what Jeremy Hooker, in his *Welsh Journal*, speaks of as 'the life we all are', which 'breathes' – both the verb and the change of tense are significant – 'itself in us' – a secret, ongoing process. Secret because it cannot be expressed.

Even so, a poem might point towards what cannot be said. Deeply interested in science though she was, she would not settle for scientific materialism. *A propos* of the cultural anthropologist David Lewis-Williams' influential *The Mind in the Cave* ('What is in our heads is in our heads, not located beyond us'): 'I liked his theory,' she wrote to me, 'but don't at all see that Lewis-Williams' reductionist personal conclusions inevitably arise from them.'

In a conversation with Fiona Owen, published in *Planet 192* about the evolutionary pioneer Alfred Russel Wallace, she speaks of the opposition popularly held to exist between religious experience and scientific discovery. 'I haven't felt,' she says, 'such an opposition.' In drawing attention to Wallace's speculative approach to his work, she suggests that perhaps scientific exploration actually begins with a kind of imagining (a kind of 'what if . . . ?'), in that sudden 'glimpsing' of a possibility that must precede the long process of reaching after fact and reason.

She shared with Wallace, both in his preoccupation with the natural world and the intense attention they both gave to it, a felt kinship with creation in all its particularity. In one of her 'farm poems', 'The Bird', she speaks of the need to feel oneself in nature – which after all one is, but only too rarely fully experiences – and the inevitable consciousness of difference between our own (self) awareness and other animals' awareness, at least as we imagine it. For me, too, animals remain a mystery. I remember two dragonflies hawking over our lawn as my wife sat holding our youngest cat, skimming, hovering, darting, flashing with bewildering speed and change of direction so that it was virtually impossible to follow them with the human eye. The little cat was entranced, ears cocked, head moving, up, down, this way and that, in concert with the dragonflies. As I might have put it, she was discovering what wonder there is simply in living. But the reality might have been wholly different.

Like Auden's 'Their Lonely Betters', 'The Bird' states a paradox: that the gift of words estranges us (and thus makes for our 'loneliness') from the very world towards which languages reaches out. For if, as Wittgenstein pointed out, the limits of language are the limits of my world, they are the limits of *my* world, not the world as it is. There *is* a life beyond language. In a short essay, 'Is a religious poem possible in the early 21st century?', written as a result of a discussion held at Bleddfa in 2004, Anne writes, 'Our deepest experiences have always been known to lie beyond words.' She recognised that language, everywhere differentiated, subject to change and even death, can never embody ultimate reality. Quoting a line ('The secret is set in the leaves') written by a 6 year-old girl at an outdoor poetry workshop, she speaks of the shock that sometimes makes us feel awe before the 'otherness' of life-forms. 'Such moments,' she wrote, 'further open us to the numinous'.

Her sensibility was essentially religious, wholly and seriously alert to life in a way rarely observed in others. For her what we call 'mystery' was not a problem to be explained away; not something that surrounds whatever it is – a sort of invisible shell – but the thing itself. A true poem, as she says herself, is analogous to mystical experience. It takes place in an inner room, a place towards which language points but can never reach, a room without a door.

For the Vaughan Association, for *Scintilla*, its championship of the life of the spirit, and for the community of friends which gradually over the years has grown out of that original foundation, we are deeply indebted to Peter Thomas and Anne Cluysenaar. I, in particular, have my own reasons to be grateful for Anne's friendship. She once told me that she didn't read much fiction. Yet, unknown to me, she had read my novel *Taking Leave*, as a result of which she then borrowed its predecessor, *Hazard's Way*, from Peter Thomas. Having learnt from my cousin Mercer that there was a third novel in existence – it was *North* – she wrote to ask how she might get hold of it. Then, somehow or other, she managed to find a copy of my first novel, *North Wall*, long out of print and virtually unobtainable.

I saw her but once a year (though, of course, we did write to one another), and I would talk to her about what I was doing, or hoped to do, and always stored up what she said, for it had to see me through the winter. Amid all the rebuffs, the discouragements and self-questionings that afflict those of us who profess the writing life, she was unfailingly supportive. She persuaded me that she believed in my work – a conviction, I have to say, not shared by many – and that made all the difference. Just what I owe to her may be judged by these few lines of a letter she wrote to me about *Evening Light* in 2009: 'I have read your new book. I am moved by it, and the range of issues it is making me think about. I want to reread it soon – I was interrupted, each time for several days, and feel I want to move through it again, more continuously, savouring the detail. I do love your work.'

Re-reading that now brings to mind some words of Jeremy Hooker's: that really it is the friends known and unknown, few though they may be, for whom one writes. Now she has gone. But I shall continue to hear, in her poems and letters, what she herself says of Henry Vaughan at the conclusion of her Introduction to the *Selected Poems* – 'the voice of a dear friend'.

PATRICIA McCARTHY

In Dublin's Fair City

to Anne Cluysenaar

As a little girl in a red velvet dress and bolero
angora-white, I might have passed you
on a city street, caught your fleeting image

in a Georgian window smudged by rain.
In the hall of a *Feis Ceoil*, I might have played
to you, my manuscript filled suddenly

with your poetry's notes as I sight-read,
then performed. The two set piano pieces
you might have heard over the judges' heads

while you danced to your digs, your pocket
rattling with a percussion of coins
for the meter and single-bar electric fire –

no women allowed on College grounds
after six o'clock. Down at the docks,
in the harbour, gangplanks must have held you,

Mail boats and Steam packet boats
storing in their holds your scholarly works
roughed in sea-crossings forwards and back.

Holyhead, Dun Laoghaire, Liverpool, Dublin . . .
the mantra on your lips four years long
and more. Neither of us would have known –

between tongue-twisters in Welsh
of porters and guards, and the boat train's clatter
past ogre-faces of cliffs carved by high tides

into unreliable coastlines – that this land
of Owain Glyndŵr, David Jones, Dylan himself
would claim you with such brutality. Anne –

through Front Gate, footsteps will cover yours
with youth and turn them into standing stones
amidst the cobbles on Trinity's square.

There you line up with Beckett, Goldsmith,
Swift, your poems etched on buildings swaying
forever to the elemental rhythms of loss.

Note:

Feis Ceoil: Classical piano competition held in Dublin.

JAY RAMSAY

Scintilla

for Anne

Suddenly: at some point near or beyond midnight, when you've been driving for longer than you can think clearly, the real reality occurs to you – simply and almost overwhelmingly

that it is all happening at once, all of it: being born, dying, falling in love, parting . . . grieving, killing, lying, laughing . . . running scared, dancing for joy, screaming aloud, starving
                     . . . as the veil tears

– all that has been held separately for the sake of sanity, clarity, individuality –

all of these brightly imaged scintillations like fragments of film gathering around a single point, a single cone, shining in this darkness

this moment, this *now* of reality that can't be uttered because it is everything

seeing that

it can only be, and only is

as all of us, one by one, choose it

Anne in Dulwich

DILYS WOOD

Anne stayed with me in a small ex-Council house I had in Dulwich, London on five or six occasions over several years. This included times when she led workshops for Second Light or gave readings and also when she was researching *Batu-Angas*, her poetry collection based on the life and work of Alfred Russel Wallace, the Victorian naturalist, whose studies of plants and animals are considered as important as Darwin's. Anne set out to study some of the actual specimens brought back from Wallace's travels and now in the Natural History Museum and also to see living specimens – I recall her setting out with some trepidation for Syon Park Butterfly House one time. She was always slightly appalled by the size of London and complicated travel but nothing would deter her when set on obtaining first-hand knowledge. Close observation was so often the beginning of a poem for her. I was aware of a huge privilege when I had Anne in the house – an early waker, she was ready for a long talk over a tray of morning tea, then over breakfast. We had to remind each other of the time, as talk was seamless. I also think, on reflection, that Anne – always one for giving – had it half in mind to 'sing for her supper', imparting the riches of her mind to a beginner poet, me, who would benefit. I benefited so much that many of the points which came up – and especially those touching on 'marginal' experiences, not explicable by reason or current knowledge – stuck in my mind and are linked with an image of Anne in bed in the back bedroom, tea tray before her, a large cashmere shawl loaned from me round her shoulders. It was chilly in that room but she was a warm body and loved the bed, which had an exceptionally soft mattress. We spoke of dispatching the bed to Wales for her. As Anne's poetry often reveals, her mind had a mystical turn and she was constantly subject to 'connections', physically experienced, with her own past life, the past life of places and (something rather different) an empathy with animals. I was probably of a more sceptical cast of mind but when Anne imparted experiences I believed absolutely. For example, she had a favourite bitch, who cured her of a migraine by intuiting where the pain was and pressing a paw to the spot. I would not have 'swallowed' that from most friends but Anne understood the connection between man and creature more profoundly than most people. She was an 'eco-poet' long before the word was dreamed up. Because the value she placed on all life was so strong she had a bone to pick with Wallace over the killing of specimens to be preserved and brought home. For most people his actions were 'in the past' and 'of his time' but I suspect Anne experienced past time, including her own childhood, as a parallel world close at hand, thin walls shifting to let her in. For someone who lived so much through spiritual experience, Anne was, as all her friends know, down to earth, earthy and practically minded – feet on the ground or she could never have coped with keeping the small-holding going. A friend so sensitive, so profoundly knowledgeable and such fun is a very great loss.

Anne, when I brought the tea-tray

to your morning pulpit of rumpled sheets,
you pulled round you that old cashmere shawl
with raggedy ends always put out for you,

when you were staying with me in Dulwich
ready for eager, desultory chat
about dogs, horses, parents, poems, instincts,

and any minor miracles, with which
your capacious memory was always full –
for instance, I forget what you called

that gentle bitch of yours, so intuitive
she cured a migraine by just touching a paw
to the pain-spot? I couldn't doubt you,

you seemed to me the purest source of knowledge
your brain buzzing with nameless things
until with tentative lips you put names

to all your daily life round the farm,
and in the woods, as you walked your pony
in the prints of Henry Vaughan's grey nag,

speaking also about that other hero,
Alfred Russel Wallace . . . How you wrestled
with his Victorian licence to kill

and preserve and bring home all those 'finds' —
all threats to life making you shake,
trying for words that keep death at bay.

And even time — minutes, hours long gone —
you liked to re-assemble, re-animate,
giving to rocks, to strata, a living soul.

How can I (but I must) link death with you?
Pure violence, a naked blade, surely
should not challenge those soft layers

with which we keep the cold out
and our thoughts in their bodily nest,
words warmed by our breath, even in

that chilly back-bedroom where ideas
were visibly white on some mornings

GRAHAM HARTILL

from Migrating Bones

But aren't they always?

and isn't this
the oldest thing

the dead being wild,
being out of control?

the spirits
heading
back to the woods?

*

that forestry beyond the ridge,
Coed Ddu,
before they felled it –

one winter day I wouldn't go in,
so dark
and thick with snow –
a vast heavy roof
and the thinnest light
in the avenues

or that dream, in the early 80's,
of ashes
whispering down the chimney –

only that –

I woke afraid –

went the long way round instead
trudging through fields of dazzling snow

*

Edward Thomas
left a feather of presence,
a sign
for anyone to follow

just calling it
reels it in
and makes it comprehensible,
manageable,
language bringing the open world
into being,
meaning
negotiation
with open light

and any agreement dependent on us
using of course
the same currency:
Trust –

*

no, not just the unconscious
but an unconscious beyond the unconscious,
the *wild*,
the fangs!
the eyes of the dog in full chase
its major joy,
the exuberance of its life

being what terror is for –
it's fight or flight

and it is finally
the mystery
of our bodies,

the brain
the darkest and most complex forest –

and what shall
we leave behind?

a new
feather?

※

Edward Thomas: *The Green Roads*

FRANK OLDING

Rhiannon

I

From the mound of wonders
I *would* see a miracle
or suffer otherwordly hurt;

two grooms I sent to catch her
on two swift steeds
but all to no avail –

the more their haste,
the further off she was
with her stallion's steady, lesiured pace.

II

Her pace no faster than before,
I saddled my own mount –
spurred his flank, gave him his head,

thought at second leap to overtake,
but came no nearer
and then, despairing, shouted "Wait for me!"

"Gladly," she said
"and had you asked the sooner,
all the better for the horse."

III

Where fair-haired May-eve boy was raised
with the colt that stood at birth,
you also nurtured colts

and despite your steady, leisured pace,
we never caught you
far, far ahead on your lead-horse;

where Rhiannon's pain was eased
by love and care,
her penance came to you.

Rhiannon

I

O orsedd y cyneddfau,
fe fynnwn weld rhyfeddod
neu oddef archoll arallfydol;

dau facwy a anfonais ar ei hôl
ar ddau farch cyflym
ond ni thyciai dim –

po fwyaf oll eu brys,
pellaf fyddai hithau wrthynt
a cherdded araf, gwastad gan ei march.

II

A'i cherdded hithau heb fod mwy na chynt,
esgynnais ar fy march fy hun –
lladd ei ystlys a'i ollwng wrth awenau,

meddwl ar yr ail naid oddiweddyd,
ond heb fod nes
ac yna, o anobaith, galw "Aros fi!"

"Yn llawen," meddai hi
"a phe baet ti wedi erchi 'nghynt,
buasai'n fwy o les i'r march."

III

Lle magwyd mab penfelyn calan Mai
a'r ebol praff a safodd yn y fan,
ebolion a fegaist tithau

ac er dy gerdded araf, gwastad,
ni lwyddwyd fyth i'th ddal
ymhell bell wrthym ar dy geffyl blaen;

lle lleddfwyd ing Rhiannon
trwy gariad ac ymgeledd,
ei phenyd hithau a ddaeth i'th ran.

TONY CURTIS

Following the Horses

At fifteen, too young to plough, he was put to harrow
With two of his father's shire horses,
Old enough and wise enough to know their own way.

Sometimes in the length of that summer
He'd even hitch a ride on the roller –
Bird song, dreaming, not a care.

That year his clenched fists on handle and reins
Chafed and blistered and calloused
Into the roughness of a man's.

Jasper and Ned made steady progress through long afternoon
To tea-time. Then over his shoulder
An approaching thunder, rumbling low and then louder

With the roar of a Wellington dragging its shadow
Over the fields that spooked both horses and boy, so he'd run
Forward to their huge, startled heads and talked them down.

The bomber skimmed over Painters Coppice, limping
Towards Hampstead Norreys, from its port engine
A pall of smoke across the trees and into the evening sky.

That night in the White Hart his father heard them say
The landing had been a close thing,
The pilot tough and skilled at twenty-three.

But Tail End Charlie, barely older than the plough-boy,
Had caught it – his shrapnelled guts held in by
The navigator's arms until the ambulance came.

Seventy years on he wonders what the ending might have been:
Air crews didn't speak of what they'd seen
Except through nods and looks and silences.

That day: the smell of turned earth, clear blue skies
Etched with dark smoke, the reek of burning oil
Silencing the birds. And the horses' wide eyes.

Henry Vaughan, Edward Lhuyd, Anne Cluysenaar & the Stones

STEVIE DAVIES

> Like me you might have held
> the weight of it, this gashed stone
> made out of slow deposits
>
> filtering down under pressure –
> something I think your mind
> would have held quite easily,
> though your time could only guess
> at the vastness of such transformations.
>
> (Anne Cluysenaar, 'Vaughan Variations', 18)

A recessive figure in a mountainous landscape, he walks an edge-lit path into obscurity. Stooping to consider some detail of green nature or rising to survey a large perspective, he's an observer always searching for something hidden within the visual. He takes an interest in the stones in his path, overhearing their pregnant silences, for stones 'hear, see, speak, / And into loud discoveries break'. An outdoor person with an intense interior life, reclusive and solitary, Henry Vaughan haunts the margins of a clamorous and bellicose world, travelling a palimpsest along unmapped but familiar pathways. He is in touch with the rhythms of nature. The dawn chorus arrests him, the plight of small birds in tempestuous weather. He observes their great migrations and small nestings, the wayside daisy that tracks the sun around the mortal day, the motion and commotion of waters in lake, stream and river, the fallen body of a tree. Often he finds himself moving through darkness or dim, occluded light, through the angled glow of a fugitive sunset. The other night, he saw eternity.

As he compulsively walks, Vaughan views in his native hills the stillness not of inert matter but of the endlessly expectant. His twin brother is a practising alchemist and Henry's mind is saturated in its mysteries. In a living universe, common stones are aspirants without pride or dissent: 'For the creatures, watching with lifted head, wait for the revelation of the sons of God.' A magical world of sympathies yearns upwards to its Creator. Angel, animal, vegetable, mineral: all is one.

> And do they so? Have they a sense
> Of ought but influence?
> Can they their heads lift, and expect,
> And groan too? . . .
>
> I would I were a stone, or tree,
> Or flower by pedigree,
> Or some poor high-way herb, or spring
> To flow, or bird to sing . . .

Creation, groaning and travailing, awaits Christ's restoration. Only man is unstable and variable, or flinty-hearted and obdurate. It dawns on Vaughan afresh, new every morning (for 'Mornings are mysteries'): everything around me is alive. This stone here, that tree, flower, stream, bird: all these are in a state of unanimous worship. This is astounding to him – but obvious and simple.

His great spiritual testament was written within a period of about ten years and published in two volumes, *Silex Scintillans* ('The Flashing Flint'), 1650 and 1655). This poetry is the fruit of mortifying defeat by his Parliamentarian enemies in the Civil Wars; it represents the enforced exile of an Anglican churchgoer from his church, a kingless Royalist. *Silex* testifies to Vaughan's passionate search for meaning in a world of desolation. The whole visible landscape, composed of the rocks from which the churches of the area were formed, becomes for those years Henry Vaughan's sacred place – or rather, the site of his quest for sanctuary. Intimations of light appear – and, as readily, fail. Bearing witness to the Father-Creator, Nature at moments bodies forth the Cosmic Christ and its very stones are fragments, in a heinous world, of an original innocence.

As Vaughan walks his hills and valleys, he carries and constantly refers to his pocket bible.

*

Take your notebook and glossary of fossils in your pocket and you can't go wrong. Walk, climb, measure, collect, catalogue.

In 1660, in the Welsh part of Shropshire, near Oswestry, is born another walker and stone-obsessed nature-observer. Edward Lhuyd is a Welsh scientist who revolutionises the study of botany, geology, palaeontology and Celtic philology. He attends Vaughan's old Oxford college, Jesus College, enlists as a soldier for another Stuart king, James II, and corresponds with Vaughan's cousin, the biographer and antiquary, John Aubrey. Lhuyd becomes, four years before the poet's death, Keeper of the Ashmolean Museum, and achieves intellectual fame by adding descriptions of all the Welsh counties to the new translation of Camden's great survey, *Britannia*.

By now it's the age of big wigs and the Royal Society. Lhuyd's portrait shows him stately, plump and huge-haired. I imagine him, however, wigless in Snowdonia, Cornwall, Ireland, scrambling over scree to winkle out rare alpine plants at height, or underground in candle-lit caves observing fossils, which he records and preserves, with his trained assistants. Edward Lhuyd investigates by systematic fieldwork and first-hand observation, cautious double-checking of data and questionnaires sent to a network of informants: 'there is no good to be done without repeated observations.' His rather wonderful letters breathe this spirit of rapt scientific enquiry.

In 1688 Lhuyd discovers the Snowdon lily, which until recently bore his name – *Lloydia serotina*. He and his assistants pack plants and stones into chests and send them on carts to Oxford. In the cold and rain of the Little Ice Age, Lhuyd on his 3,000 mile trek abandons the atrocious post roads for paths leading to quarries, pits, mine workings. In coalfields he finds 'fern branches in the coal slate'. Lhuyd coins the names *siliquastra* and *glossopetrae* for shark teeth. He trains quarrymen to recognise fossils in the strata.

Lhuyd calls his finds 'figured stones' or 'formed stones', as against the 'inscribed stones' of the ancient monuments he also visits and documents. Doubtless his pocket bible is there in his luggage; he doesn't question the overarching divine design. But he's recognisably a modern, practising a 'new science of Natural History'. Lhuyd's is a feet-on-the-ground Enlightenment concept of happiness: 'I understand by happynesse a serenity of minde & disposition to do good.' Though doubtless the two men never met, Lhuyd visits Vaughan's haunts, the River Usk and Llangorse Lake, observing the wildlife and fossil record of the Brecon Beacons. From Usk Lhuyd writes of discovering, in limestone south of Abergavenny, 'new species of Glossopetra . . . on top of a high mountain called Blorens near Aber Gavenni'. At Carreg Cennen in Carmarthen, he finds marine fossils on the walls and roof of caves:

> Now although I can readily grant that the Deluge [Noah's Flood] might have cast marine bodies into these & any other caves: yet can I not allow that it could ever fasten them to their . . . roofs & sides: and that they should be sunk so deep from the top, is the difficulty of the former objection . . . I leave it to your self & other unprejudiced observers to consider of their origin.

*

In April 1995 the poet Anne Cluysenaar notices, in a stream near Scethrog, a particular stone, a rather odd one, for marks seem to have been carved in it. Later she'll call it the 'gashed stone', which becomes an object of meditation for her. 'Gashed' implies violent pain. But stones can't feel – can they?

Anne walks in the footsteps both of Vaughan and Lhuyd – the mystic and the scientist. She's saturated in the findings of modern geology, evolutionary thought and cosmology. Turning over the gashed stone in her hands, Anne takes its heft, reads with her fingertips its texture and muses over its possible history or histories. Stone, she knows, encodes messages from distant epochs: eras of sedimentation, glaciation, attrition by water, pressure through aeons of geological time. What might Henry Vaughan have made of the gashed stone, with its hieroglyphic-seeming writing? She carries it away with her, a token of her quest, and shows it to us at a gathering at Brecon Museum to commemorate the tercentenary of Henry Vaughan's death. From this celebration the Vaughan Association grows, and the journal *Scintilla*. Anne's poem-cycle, 'Vaughan Variations', is published in *Timeslips: New & Selected Poems* (1997).

How old is our earth? Vaughan measured its antiquity in biblical rather than geological time. 'The poor world,' says Rosalind in *As You Like It*, 'is almost six thousand years old.' Bishop James Ussher in the seventeenth century calculated the date of the Creation as nightfall on 22 October 4004 BC. Between Ussher and the geologist Charles Lyell, time stretched to over 300,000 years. When Anne Cluysenaar comes to Brecon, she brings with her a modern reckoning of 4.5 billion years and a deep fascination with geological time: how to feel and voice it. She considers, in troubled wonderment, 'the short pulse of our time' ('Drawing Breath'); 'the earth's surfaces, riding and dipping . . . / Ice-ages and deserts and seas that will come' ('Natural History').

In the 'Vaughan Variations', Anne seeks, with the unique empathy and honesty of her poesis, to enter Vaughan's mental landscape and to survey hers by its light. What has Vaughan's arcane journey to say to us now, three centuries after his death? She has his poetry by heart. Not a nuance escapes her. Each of the twenty-three variations opens with a ripple of quotation, a Vaughan epigraph. But these gleanings are rarely the famous lines, such as we all remember: not 'Bright shoots of everlastingness' or 'They are all gone into the world of light!' The epigraphs are wayside moments of meditation, off the popular mind's beaten track, intimacies between Anne herself and Vaughan himself: 'sense, / Things distant doth unite' (5); 'Accept this salmon' (7); 'Hath flesh no softness now? Mid-day no light?' (8).

Anne starts in Llansantffraed Churchyard, beside Vaughan's tombstone, which in 1995 lies cracked, greened over with lichen and ivy, 'Broken across "sepulchrum" and / "voluit"'. Looking round, she wonders if, 'nearby, / there's matter that held you, and still / lives on. But never you again.' Thinking of him:

> near your grave, has made you too real,
> like a parent after his death.
> My temples ache as if with tears.
> It's a betrayal to say 'you'
> to the self your words breathe in me.

The 'Vaughan Variations' bear witness to the virtuosity of close reading. The words remain the same; our interpretations are manifold and fluid. To read Anne's reflections reminds us that poetry 'flies and flows', hiddenly, privately, from one life to another, through generations. The epigraph to the eighteenth variation is from Vaughan's 'Vanity of Spirit': 'To search myself, where did I find / traces, and sounds of a strange kind . . .'. Her mind tracks back to the 'gashed stone'. Whether it was inscribed by a human being or a plough, her attention to the stone and its markings invests it with mediatorial status. 'A slanting light, the light / archaeologists love, reaches / the stone in your hands', she writes. Whose hands? Vaughan's? Lhuyd's? Anne's? Mine? The cycle of variations puzzles at the distinction between 'I' and 'you', the streaming of one voice into another – in a world of recurrent loss and mourning.

'Never you again.' And Anne too is gone. Many of her poems were elegiac. She had an extraordinary gift for friendship; friends' deaths sent her to the periphery of the social world. Anne recognised Vaughan as a poet of the margin, his inner world like his scenery 'edge-lit', off-centre, in retreat. She responded to his schismatic self – half a pair of sundered twins, a speaker of twin tongues, one (the Welsh) stigmatised. Has-been and anachronism, he was no more and no less than 'a man holding a stone'.

Vaughan, as Anne felt, addresses our urgent concerns. Environmentalism. The inviolability of the child. Wars of religion. Reading Vaughan, we intuit a closeness to the territory of Gaia, biogeochemistry and the Green sense of the whole earth as one complex and interactive biosphere. Vaughan's outsiderliness, his courage in thinking anomalously, speaks to us as it spoke to Anne Cluysenaar, of the unaccommodated heart, vagrant and truthful at the edge of a fragmented culture. His friends had all gone into the world of light.

> There was nothing to see but
> the edge of an empty field and
> a woman standing at the edge
>
> ('Vaughan Variations', 16)

HILARY LLEWELLYN-WILLIAMS

Like Them that Dream

They that sowed in tears will sing when they reap (Psalm 126)
i.m. Anne Cluysenaar 1.11.14

All your journeys led to your final day.
A day full of sun: the last of summer waving
farewell as it dawdled over the hills,
fingered the fading leaves and let them fall,

strolled along streets and sideroads,
glancing in our gardens
at papery hydrangeas and pale pinched roses,
sliding round corners

to creep in windows and splash warm light on a wall,
deepening all colour. One last, long note
at the end of a symphony. That afternoon

I got the mower out, the manual one I use,
and shoved its blades through damp grass.
The last cut of the year. It snagged and stalled
and chewed up chunks of earth but I persevered:

this, I sensed, would be the last chance. Last chance
to gather husks from the bean canes
and clear the rotting apples from the path
and weed the veg beds ready for winter planting.

How did you spend your day at the little farm?
With the animals, standing with them in the shade
by the forest eaves? In the kitchen, looking out to the sun,
planning for winter? Thinking of spring, of poems?

Forever looking forward, that's what we do
while we keep breathing and pumping the blood around:
setting out for the future moment, the next hard thing
till the future stops. *Carrying seed for the sowing.*
We shall be *like them that dream*

when our captivity shall be *turned again*
like a stream diverted, surprisingly
and all at once, flowing now in a new direction
into the dry ground, into the empty spaces –

and yes, suddenly facing another way
we'll see what the departing summer sees
as it slips from the hilltop and the rocky places:
the whole world rolling backwards, away from us.

You left the world to its motion, not intending
to leave, but always ready to start. Joining
the tail-end of the harvest celebration –
weeping, singing, carrying your sheaves.

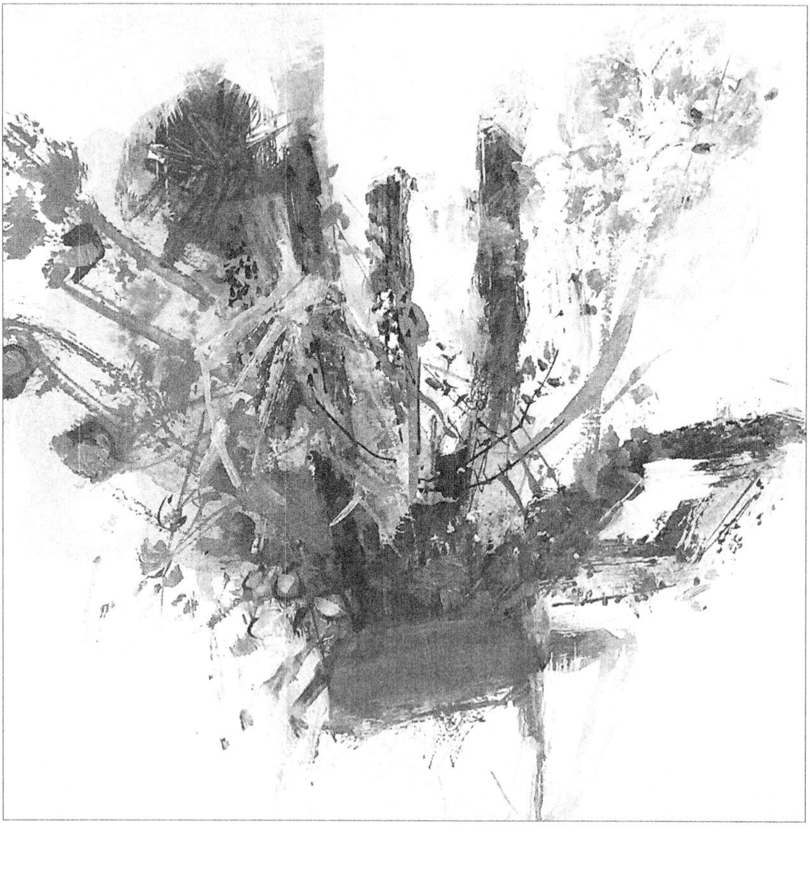

JOHN FREEMAN

Time Perpetually Revolving

A sequence for Anne Cluysenaar

1: Refectory Wellhead

She was the subtlest centre of attention
in my first memory of her over lunch
in a half-empty college refectory
after a morning of forgotten papers.
There were ten or a dozen of us with her;
most of them already knew each other
and were a band of friends, fellow-spirits,
fellow-professionals with a new ideal.
But this was relaxation time, laughter
and easy chat as well as longer speeches.
As they spoke each one disclosed herself –
or himself, but they were mostly women –
and I liked them all but in the others
saw as you might see in a friend without
making too much of it, or passing judgement,
some lack or limitation all their talent
was framed by, leaving them only human.
And Anne herself was never less than human,
but without seeking to impose herself
she spread, along with appreciation
of her companions and what they were saying –
her palpable attention, you could feel,
enhanced for all of us what was spoken –
an authority and benevolence
that didn't need to be announced or mentioned.
It emanated from her and filled up
the gathering with distinction she gave it
from depths and heights beyond most of us,
intuited within her, and a balance
we lacked so that whatever limitations

she may have had were somehow not disabling.
She was the one, therefore, who could empower
that gathering, touch an *ad hoc* group of us
over a modest lunch in a plain room –
but it had daylight, floor-to-ceiling windows –
with a magic and a faith in our potential,
as separate consciousnesses, and together,
to start a movement like a sudden freshet
bursting up out of a hillside after rain
which flows in to a river, and still flows,
as what she started at that weekend meeting
augments a current flowing decades later.

2: Team Away-Days

Once a year – how many times? Not many –
we gathered at Anne's and Walt's smallholding.
The preparations at the shops and markets
and in our kitchens were part of the event,
the approach to it, the anticipation.
People shared cars and arrived together.
There was the untidiness of parking,
greeting, milling round, getting in the way,
taking things out to the long table
on the terrace overlooking the valley
and the soft hills opposite. A perfect view,
even lovelier in the mild sunshine.
That's what memory retains, perfection,
not the build-up nor the dismantling after.
We have such an instinct for paradise
that the mind preserves without even trying
moments which approximate to heaven
or seem just about to attain it in
the next mouthful, the next thoughtful exchange, next
sweep of the gaze round the semi-circle
of the panorama spread out like a feast.
And there was Walt, good-natured and discreet,
friendly but staying in the background, busy.
I knew why we had been gathered here,

not by Anne, but with her generous help:
to make us feel so happy and expansive
we couldn't help volunteering ideas
for the year ahead of shared hard labour
which we ourselves would have to carry out.
I saw it coming, fell for it, didn't care.
Those years of daily grind are long gone by.
But I recall as if it were yesterday
that approach to a perfect happiness
which seemed always about to become complete
under Anne's presiding presence, like Walt's,
discreet, understated, always genial,
her wide-ranging intelligence, her learning
worn lightly, but always manifested,
like the empowering vitality
of the life of animals and plants round us –
the chickens below the steep drop from the terrace,
special breeds, picturesque, protected by wire
from foxes which had claimed at least one victim,
the horses in the stables, and in the woods
as we all knew, having read Anne's poems
and heard her read them to us, sometimes deer.

3: Leaning on a Bridge

Who else was there that time, and where was it,
that spacious house by a little river
in the country where several of us tutors
went to write and share ideas for teaching?
I remember a polished wooden table
in the library where we sat and talked,
greenness and quiet all around the house.
Spring, I think, but perhaps early summer.
And all this comes back from reading
Anne's poem about leaning on a bridge
with a poet looking at a river,
not the event I'm suddenly seeing,
the photograph I took of her leaning
with a different colleague on a bridge

with her back to the camera looking
into the river, her presence substantial
and the unconscious pose almost comic,
some kind of jacket, well-filled blue jeans,
but effortlessly dignified and gracious.
A memory of her as if retreating –
whereas in my last recollection,
sitting at the reception in the pub
at Peter's funeral, she looks at me,
her face never in all the years I knew her
more majestic nor more clear and bonny,
talking of how she'd miss Peter's phone-calls
in which they urged each other to new projects.
How much she took and gave in conversation
with poets, scholars, all like-minded people.
I drove back from that half-forgotten meeting
to a hospital appointment – trouble
with a persistent ear infection which
now seems minor, though it blighted a summer –
and saw in the middle of a green lawn
a brilliant bullfinch standing, the colours
of Anne's brick-red jacket and her denims.
It comes to me – the river was the Usk.

4: Artist in Residence, Spirit in Exile

That wide clear forehead, those clear blue eyes. The face
wholesome, neither florid nor pale, open.
White hair pulled not severely but neatly back.
That thoughtful and quite deep, womanly voice
with an accent to my ear more Yorkshire
than anything. She must have acquired it
during her years there in what must have been
her prime, teaching and pioneering,
writing poetry and doing research,
and at the same time keeping a farm with Walt.
And yet before that, French her first language,
exiled with her Belgian painter father.
If she picked up any Irish from her years

at TCD I never noticed it. And then
her long Indian summer, her long autumn
ablaze with colour, friendships and achievements,
at work in Cardiff, teaching M.A. students,
and at home in Henry Vaughan's Vale of Usk,
and Alfred Wallace's. Always learning
new things, pursuing the spirit of place,
homeless as she deeply felt herself to be,
the tutelary spirits she encountered –
the Vaughan twins, the Mabinogion –
she became one with, and for us is one of.

5: Migrations

I pick up a book of verse whose author
I had known for thirty years and more
when she died suddenly six months ago.
The poem that falls open moves back in time
a decade or so, a herd of cows dispersed,
then by way of tangible siltstone
visualises the reality
of how this same landscape must have been
when it was under sea, a period
so long ago the noughts are meaningless
to the imagination, the Silurian.
But in the poem she never leaves her reader
without something to see or touch or hear,
and comes back to the present and the future –
the image of herself for a whole
long hot August afternoon watching,
as she tells us, through binoculars, a hatching
of Clouded Yellows, 'the vehement zigzag
of wings'. 'And yet', she says, 'by winter, all
will be dead'. As she was, by last winter.
Reading her poem brings her back to me,
alive, in a composite portrait of her
as she was across the years I knew her,
and as I've thought in grieving of her since.
With the help of her marvellous poem,

moving backwards and forwards in time
with such assurance, I suddenly
see an image which has been gestating
for weeks through other meditations,
ready to hatch at last, of time like cards
in the hands of an ambidextrous dealer,
being cascaded evenly from one
hand to the other and back again,
each moment a card, our contemplation
moving lightly backward and forward through them,
evenly spaced, the corner of each showing
as it follows and is followed in succession,
all of the past and all the future present
all the time, perpetually revolving,
with Anne's face steady in my mind's eye, like
an image given back by moving water.

February-June, 2015

Note: As far as I can remember and ascertain, I first met Anne Cluysenaar at a conference in Manchester in 1983 out of which the Verbal Arts Association was formed, under her chairmanship. I was on the committee of the VAA and travelled to Sheffield several times for committee meetings. In 1990 Anne joined the Creative Writing team of teachers at Cardiff University. The first three poems in my sequence refer to these associations. The Peter referred to in the third poem is of course Peter Thomas, co-founder with Anne of *Scintilla*.

DAVID GRUBB

Astonishings

September is a good time for this;
they come out of the ground stuffed
with summer wheat and barley and sometimes
berries and bits of shell, butter shine and the silence
is like a stream of meteors as we lay them down gently
and do not want to tell those who will not believe.

Sometimes we are not quite sure what we have;
broken wings are normal but what have they done
to the beautiful legs and the music has gone cold
and the people who know about such things are
evidently terrified by what they now think they hear
which is actually another kind of silence.

The police arrive and they tape off the place
and the local media are told to shut it and a crowd
assembles in the inevitable rain that drips silver;
they call it news whereas it is older than words
and the God Men will invent extra silences which
they always do to enhance what cannot be said.

These things are what my father calls Astonishings;
moments when you enter future or as you run into the
orchard you see yourself in the nearest tree or when a
man walks through our village looking for a house that
is no longer; he should have been here years ago and
lived and died but he still has all this to do.

STEVIE KRAYER

You have one missed message

October. The lane is slimed
with pikastix twigs.
On this windless foggy morning
a corner-of-the-eye movement:
out of the hacked hedge
pokes a single naked splint
of nettle, dangling
a caught oak leaf from its tip.

When nothing else moves, why
does this stalk dance
so frantically, flapping its leaf
like a folk-dancer's kerchief
or a clown's hand waggling
a goodbye? It's as if
I'd just missed the take-off –
the last bird leaving.

JOHN BARNIE

Evening in Winter

Sitting in a chair having a cat-nap
while the cat naps on my lap,
and the wood fire ticks and Beethoven's

Fourth eddies and swirls around
the room's walls, and outside
the cold in a mean compaction of envy

freezes the ground, turns poor birds
on twigs into brown feather dusters
and the stars glitter in clusters

beyond art, beyond life, beyond
the slow congenial burning of the fire
can't be bad, I reason, half

sleepily talking to the cat, who
propping his head on the armrest,
very slowly, closes his eyes.

Happiness

If you want happiness I'd say it's where
tobogganists slide in a tumble of arms and legs

and there's nothing to do but scream and laugh
as more flakes winnow down

and light fades and crows flag to roost
in the iron branches of the trees.

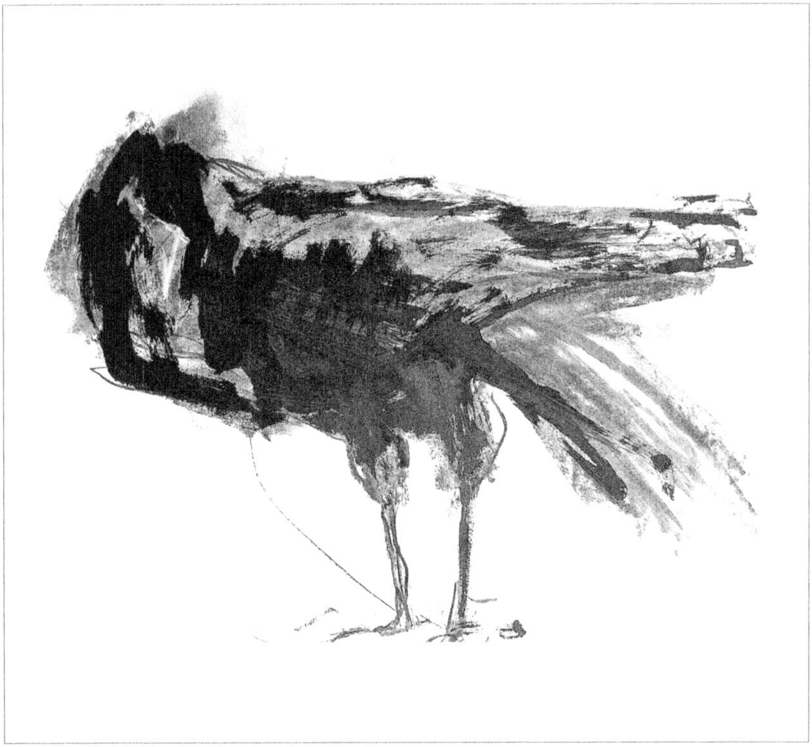

KATE FOLEY

For Anne Cluysenaar
Poet and Quaker: stabbed to death November 2014

You have been folded
into the luminous grass,
while the leaves

do what they've always done
and the small brown birds
whose voices you had to write

still sing.

A paradox –
you might have found
some words

simple as water
to rinse the terrible
stain of your death.

If we could we'd lean towards you,
share your silence
as you shared yours with us.

All we can do is sit
in the gathered Meeting
of the fields and words you loved.

HILARY DAVIES

By the Dark Lake

The geese rise in the night.
They cry beneath the moon.
Out on the water a sound like snakes
Slides nearer, and black life
Breaks under the pontoon.
Dear God, we came here for quietude,
Hope in silence,
But the dark gives no gift, no prayer.

Look at the moon in her copper serenity,
Loosing the veils of immortality,
Yet my soul is not in her carriage:
It is trapped in the reedbeds,
Far from her promises,
And the gleam of the lamprey is close.

We are never prepared for this –
Even grief's antechambers ring unfamiliar –
Never prepared for the dark lake,
For the boat with its sharp wake
Skimming across the water towards us,
For the immovable sorrow at the land's edge
Where the waves flicker,
Where at the two worlds' crossroads
Two mighty shadows meet.

JOHN POWELL WARD

Bereavement

Why is this carpet out of place?
Why isn't the floor lamp where it was?
Why isn't she where she was?

Mirrors bend across pictures. The dog,
cooker, chairs, fill vacated space.
Trees and the house abut differently.

Years are afterthought, a mere late addition,
waiting for what mode of being-one
is now strange parallel to earthly view.

This void has gone surreal and fixed
at once. My huge ache is so
everywhere it is numb; I lack comparison.
Even tears freeze, as though for later use.

Written for the poet's late wife, but it can gladly appear here in honour of Anne too, for her friendship and supreme qualities.

Living on in Life-Praise

SUSAN BASSNETT

After the shock of a death, after the grief of the funeral comes the mundane yet fearsome task of disposing of the belongings of the departed one. Sometimes this involves clearing a whole house, sorting through decades of the paraphernalia accumulated over a lifetime, sometimes it is less onerous, but it always involves contact with the ephemera of another person's existence, with the beads, trinkets, scraps of paper, photographs, glasses cases, plants, stones, ornaments, in short, with all the memorabilia that no longer mean anything to anyone, because they were collected by and saved and meaningful only for someone who no longer exists.

With a writer, the task also involves notebooks, reams of paper, drafts, perhaps a filing cabinet or two, and always books, shelf after shelf of books, some thick with dust, others pristine and possibly never yet read. And how to dispose of books in the twenty-first century, when libraries are replacing hard copies of texts that are now available on screen, when schools and universities refuse bequests of books because of the cost of cataloguing them, when society is moving away from print, when we are all caught up in a cultural revolution as great as the shift from memory to book that happened five hundred years ago, when the advent of the printing press changed the world?

I am the Executor and Literary Executor named in Anne's last will and testament, so there have been papers to sign and decisions to take in the months since her death, but I put off the task of sorting the books and papers for as long as I could. There is something so final about taking books down from shelves and packing them into cases to be sent – where? I believe hers will be going abroad, to locations where books are still needed, in countries where war and poverty have devastated towns and villages but where the desire to learn is strong. Education, as Anne always believed, is the way out of misery and oppression, and it may be that some of her books find their way to refugee camps or remote villages where the internet is still a distant dream and being able to hold a book is the stepping stone to a better future.

As I sorted through the thousands of books, packing away hundreds of novels, anthologies, scientific works, illustrated books about wildlife and birds, books on religion, medicine, physics, stylistics, literary theory, books in English and books in French, battered old books from Anne's childhood, I began to bring certain people to mind for specific items. To someone, I could donate the poetry pamphlets Anne must have collected in her Dublin days; to my son, books on archaeology and myth, along with volumes of Jung, Levi-Strauss, Joseph Campbell; to another person, books on geology; to another, books on Celtic spirituality; to another, books on astronomy; to another, a selection of contemporary poets. I filled boxes for the anonymous recipients, and a few boxes to take away and distribute to those people I knew would be grateful for the gift. What was both moving and awe-inspiring was the sheer range of subjects combined with the evidence of how carefully those books had been read, the hand-written marginalia, the endless tiny scraps of paper marking topics and pages, the notes pushed in between pages. Anne was an intellectual omnivore, and her books span the arts, humanities and sciences. She did what all writers do, which is to build up collections of relevant books for whatever project she was engaged in, hence I could see the books she had used for her edition of Henry Vaughan, for *Time-Slips*, for *Batu-Angas*, for *Migrations*, and in the filing cabinet were articles, notes, press cuttings, all the paraphernalia of intensive research. And at the same time, she never lost sight of the natural world, the world of dogs, birds, plants, horses, the stars above her, the sunsets and sunrises and the whole tapestry of living things with which she was constantly in touch. Anne was certainly an intellectual, but she was also, by training and temperament a countrywoman, a lover of the natural world.

Over our forty-year friendship, we exchanged a lot of work in draft form, and in more recent years Anne sent me an increasing number of poems. In her sixties and seventies she was writing better poetry than ever, and so prolifically. *Touching Distance*, the collection that came out in 2014, is only a small selection of the dozens of diary poems that she produced over a roughly five year period. What seems to have happened is that she became increasingly fascinated by the processes of memory and ageing, analysing herself, as it were, and she also met and exchanged ideas with congenial people locally. In one of her emails enclosing new poems, she wrote: 'The Second Light women are a great pleasure, honest and various and writing the sort of poetry I can fully admire – though not in one 'style', always pursuing real experiences'.

In another email, responding to something I had written on translation, she wrote: 'As a poet, I am wanting new forms, new tones, to reach me through translation . . . I am especially struck by what you said about translation as a form of remembering. Deeply moved by that. A wide-ranging thought'.

Translation was important for Anne, because she always moved between languages. As a native French speaker for whom English was the second language, a point she always insisted be emphasised, she understood the aporia, the lacunae that have to be negotiated through translation. The translator is always seeking to make sense, to convey that which cannot be reproduced identically. When we first met, our earliest conversations were about translation, about how translation tests one's limits, since what can be expressed in one way in one language has necessarily to be expressed differently in another language. The question she used to return to was whether this means that we occupy different worlds when we use our different languages, whether the bilingual person is always seeking an explanation for the inexplicable.

For Anne, translation meant far more than linguistic transfer; it involved reconfiguring ideas, forms, images that came from a variety of sources. She drew on so many sources for her poetry, which is what makes reading her work such a rich experience. I thought I had read all her works, but then on one of the shelves, I found a little pamphlet of her poems, price one shilling and sixpence, published in 1967 and entitled *A Fan of Shadows*. There are just six poems, 'Orpheus' 'Petrarch', 'The Fawn', 'Figures', 'Sea', and 'Epithalamium', but already we can see the major strands that were to run through her subsequent writing. The note on 'Orpheus' tells us that 'the third verse alludes to the cosmic theory of continuous creation', the note on 'Sea' states that 'recurrence and change can make us doubt the value of what recurs and changes'. 'Figures' uses the Persian ghazal form, but the hills that 'flow up unmoving / from slower waves of grass / to make the horizon balance' are the hills of the Lake District, and so Persian poetry blends with Wordsworthian echoes. In this tiny collection we can see her developing interest in both the scientific and the spiritual, her reflections on personal experiences combined with a powerful sense of history and continuity, her willingness to experiment with new forms, reaching out across cultural boundaries.

Many years later, in 2010, Anne wrote a long poem based on the *Epic of Gilgamesh* that was included in her *Migrations* collection. Entitled 'Clay', it is prefaced by two sentences, a dedication:

In memory of a student scribe,
Mesopotamia c.2070 BC

and a line by Edward Thomas,

'the living past, the dying present'.

Originally entitled 'He Who Saw the Deep', the first version was much longer than the final one, and after she had sent it to me, Anne wrote that she was completely reworking it 'thanks to some detailed comments from Jerry Hooker – I asked him to comment, feeling unsatisfied with it though still excited by it – it seemed to have become more a mobile than a palimpsest. What he said confirmed that and I am now trying to move it nearer to the latter'.

What Anne was doing with this poem is typical of her technique: she is rereading, that is 'translating' an ancient epic which has a universal theme, that of fearing and trying to defy death, which she combines with personal memories and with her own spiritual quest. Here, as an example of how she worked, are the two versions of just one section of the poem, where it is evident how she pared down and focussed the memory of herself as a child:

'If in the silver mirror
you should see yourself,' she said,
'give her something you think she needs'
Rising as if through water, a girl
in a moth-holed jersey – the holes
my mother embroidered with flowers –
holds our both her hands to me.
But I've nothing I feel she needs.
I find myself holding out
my hands, till our fingers meet.
She steps towards me, she steps
 right into me, out of sight.
A wholeness I had forgotten.

(Unpublished draft)

As if through water, a girl
in a moth-holed jersey – the holes
my mother embroidered with flowers –
holds out both her hands to me.
But I've nothing I feel she needs.
I find myself stretching out
my hands, till our fingers meet.
She steps toward me, she steps
right into me, out of sight.

(*Migrations* p.59)

In the preface to 'Clay', Anne explains that the *Epic of Gilgamesh* first became important to her in her teens 'and certain aspects seemed to find an echo in subsequent experiences'. She tells us that she recently discovered that her mitochondrial DNA indicates descent from a woman living some 10,000 years ago in what is now Syria. I remember when she received that news, and how excited – and mystified – she was by it. Her preface concludes: 'It is with the thought of her world that my poem ends – a world before writing in which tales may have been told which later found an echo in one or another written version of the *Epic*'.

The opening poem in *A Fan of Shadows* is dedicated to Anne's mother, Sybil. 'Orpheus' is a short, beautiful poem that I see as encapsulating how Anne thought. As we read the poem, always with the myth of Orpheus in mind, it becomes clear that Anne is writing about poetry itself, about the role of the poet to show us that despite death, there is a constant process of rebirth and continuity in the universe. This is why Anne had no difficulty in accepting both the religious and the scientific, for the key to both is the acceptance of mystery and the desire to reach out for deeper awareness. Of course she had Richard Dawkins' work on her bookshelves, but she was able to do what he cannot, that is to 'translate' between the world of scientific discovery and the world of the numinous. The soul of the poet searches, she writes in the opening lines of 'Orpheus', 'down resisting thought for the dark / Centre which no song expresses':

>   There, unlit by time,
>   Our axle of change and growth
>   Revolves on a point of creation.
>   There, for us, is death.

The third verse moves on from that darkness:

>   Constantly flowing, like a poem
>   from the mind's vanishing-point,
>   an atom is born of each atom
>   To sustain time's light.

Yes, there is death, but there is also the everlasting renewal of matter, as each atom is born of another atom, and there is also the everlasting renewal of poetry across time and space. The poem concludes with four lines that remind us why this poem was dedicated to Anne's beloved mother, whose death had such a profound impact on her that, as she once told me, she was unable to listen to music for several years because of the pain of her loss:

> Though she is dead, she was,
> And became herself through time.
> Her meaning lives in life-praise,
> And at the point of creation.

Citing those lines now, in the aftermath of the sorting out of the books and papers of a beloved friend and gifted poet, I read them as about both the mother and the daughter, about Sybil Hewat and Anne Cluysenaar Jackson, whose meaning does indeed live in 'life-praise.'

July 2015

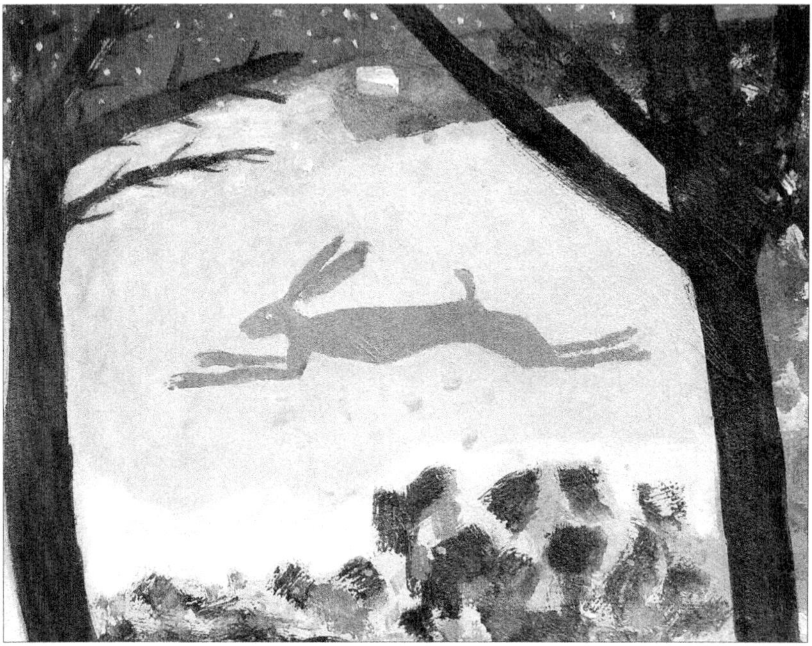

A Poet, a Theologian and a Rabbit ('for us, metaphorical'): A Reminiscence and Two Poems

BONNIE THURSTON

The Reminiscence
In November, 2009 I gave a retreat for the Society of the Sacred Cross at Tymawr near Monmouth, Wales. Part of its context was the (as it proved) fatal illness of the (then) Superior, Mother Mary Jean. Part was a rabbit which was discussed at some length on a day spent with Anne. Subsequently, we each wrote a poem about that rabbit. The following journal excerpts frame the poems, and I hope in some mysterious way speak to the tragedy of Anne's death.

November 23, 2009
After cutlery washing up at lunch and between gales of rain, I went out for a walk. On the path up to Michaelgarth there was a good sized rabbit having a wash and ear scratch. It was brown underneath with heavy, black outer fur. I wondered why it didn't respond to my approach, then realized it had no eye on my side: pink flesh on both sides, a slit where the eye should have been. I watched a while, then walked to its other side. No eye there either.

A large, adult, very blind rabbit. When I clucked my tongue, it crouched down and put its ears back, but didn't move. Its heart beat fast and sides moved with its breathing. I walked on, but came back twice to check on it. Still there and crouched down. I was sorry I'd made noise. It would have been interesting to watch it wash longer. But how does a blind rabbit make its way in the world? Achieve adulthood?

On my way into the house, the small, elegant gray cat that stays with M. Mary Jean came trotting around the old print house with a dead mouse in its mouth. Nature in its darker, starker aspects.

November 24, 2009
Listening to M. Mary Jean this morning and how she feels this terrible illness is about the Lord's healing . . . about how important it is to link her pain with

THE PAIN (Christ on the Cross, God). I realized I was in the presence of deep and genuine holiness. I was deeply humbled and deeply grateful, experienced this theme of the suffering cosmos, the blind rabbit, the holy, suffering nun, the sense that somehow it is all bound up and redeemed in the broken hearted God. 'God has dealt with our failure by himself becoming a failure in Jesus Christ and so healing it from the inside.'[1]

November 26, 2009

I realized this morning that my encounter with the rabbit made the retreat possible. Seeing the blind rabbit in its total vulnerability completely broke me open and that broken open-ness . . . has been at work in the retreat. It is the broken-openness of Christ on the cross. I'm not saying this well, but the rabbit and the retreat are closely linked.

Anne Cluysenaar told me of diseased rabbits on their farm. The animal people said not to kill them. If they are diseased and recover, they pass on their immunity. She thought my rabbit might be one of the recovered ones. If broken-ness and fragility can recover, it will have a powerful immunity to pass on.

I had a magical time with Anne. She arrived a little after 11, and we went to Monmouth for lunch at a lovely place she knew. As it was American Thanksgiving we ate a full meal: wine, pasta with prawns, green salad, sticky toffee pudding, coffee (a really *good* cup). Conversation was *wonderful* and ranged over perception, poetry, food, animals. It was a sort of home coming to be with her. As I said to her, I'll be able to live a long time on this day.

Would Melangell have been holier had her rabbit been blind?[2]

Oh Lord, I am your small, blind rabbit, having a wash and scratching my ears at the edge of a green field while all the world around me is filled with danger and terrors. But for your watch care, I am totally vulnerable. 'Hide me under the shadow of thy wings.' When God came among us in vulnerability, we killed him. In the small brown rabbit I saw the beating heart of Christ on the cross.

---

1 Maria Boulding, *Gateway to Hope: An Exploration of Failure* (London: Collins/Fount Paperbacks, 1985) 9.
2 St. Melangell was a beautiful, Irish noblewoman who went to Wales for a life of prayer. Hunting on his own land, Prince Brochwel pursued a hare into a bramble thicket where he found Melangell praying, and the hare hiding in the folds of her gown. He called off his dogs and gave her the land for sanctuary. 'Her way of life was such that wild hares surrounded her as though they had been tame.' So says the introduction of the collection of poems about St. Melangell edited by Anne Cluysenaar and Norman Schwenk, *The Hare that Hides Within* (Cardigan: Parthian, 2004) ix-x.

The Poems

St. Melangell's Rabbits

At the end of green field
beyond the protection
of tall grass, hedgerow,
the rabbit was grooming,
paws at work on face, ears,
brown body fur already sleek.
I drew much too close.
The wee beast never paused
in the work of washing,
having only pink slits
in place of ebony eye beads.
I looked on a long time
then clucked my tongue.
The rabbit drew down,
flattened its ears.
Our hearts beat fast,
our bodies bellows
wary with waiting,
both knowing ours a world
that crucifies weakness.

Watchful St. Melangell,
beckon and draw us all,
blind, vulnerable creatures
beneath the hem
of the healing garment.[3]

(Bonnie Thurston)

---

[3] The poem appears in Bonnie Thurston, *Belonging to Borders* (Collegeville, MN: Liturgical Press, 2011), 76-77.

It began with a rabbit bending

for Bonnie Thurston

It began with a rabbit bending
her ears down, to wash them,
on a misty, November morning.

While you described her to me
I imagine you stepping closer,
as if you were both in Eden,
neither frightening nor frightened.

It seemed courteous to speak, so you did.
Her answer? To turn a head
with startling signs of survival –
pink skin for eyes, healed over.

So here we were, two humans,
theologian, poet, discussing
a rabbit who certainly lives
with reduced options. But lives.

Ever since, I find myself touched
by three rabbits. A rabbit
greeting the dawn. A rabbit
who must have developed her senses.
A rabbit, for us, metaphorical.[4]

(Anne Cluysenaar)

---

4 The poem appears in Anne Cluysenaar, *Migrations* (Blaenau Ffestiniog, Gwynedd: Cinnamon Press, 2001) 86.

BONNIE THURSTON

Broaching Distances

Anne Cluysenaar (+2014)

It is not so much
the horror of the how,
but the wrongness
of her absence
that wounds,
she who was
so alive to the who
and the where,
brought the gift
of being present.
Not elsewhere,
completely here,
her attentiveness
substantive,
her perceptivity
glowing matter
in a gaseous universe.

Her *transitus* caused
a hair line fracture
in the tectonic plates
from which
her individuated
vitality invisibly,
but actually seeps
in minute free fall
toward whatever else
there is, where ever
else the light of her
looking might shine.

GRAHAM HARRIS

The Usk Conservation and Environmental Group held a commemorative evening on Wednesday July 22nd to celebrate the life of Anne Cluysenaar. The evening commenced at 7pm at the Owain Glyndwr Field, Maryport Street, Usk, where a ceramic plaque, designed and made by Ned Hayward, was erected, and wild roses were planted. There was a reading by Graham Harris, secretary / treasurer of the Environmental Group, followed by readings from poets and friends of Anne.

Photograph by Graham Harris, with thanks.

CONTRIBUTORS

Acknowledgements and Permissions

The Vaughan Association would like to thank all those who have kindly and generously donated towards this memorial issue.

MEREDITH ANDREA has two poetry pamphlets, *Grasshopper Inscriptions* (Flarestack 2006) and *Organon* (Knives Forks and Spoons 2011) and, with Fiona Owen, the poetic conversation *Screen of Brightness* (Cinnamon, 2013). She has co-edited Flarestack Poets since 2008.

RUTH BIDGOOD lives in mid-Wales. Her collection *Time Being* (Seren, 2009) won the Roland Mathias Award 2011. Her most recent one is *Above the Forests* (Cinnamon Press, 2012). It was jointly launched with Matthew Jarvis's *Ruth Bidgood* (UWP, 2012).

JOHN BARNIE's latest book is a memoir, *Footfalls in the Silence* (Cinnamon Press). A new collection of poems, *Wind Playing with a Man's Hat* will appear in October 2016 (also from Cinnamon).

SUSAN BASSNETT is a writer and academic, specialising in comparative literature and poetry translation. She has written extensively about translation, literature and creativity. Besides her academic writing, she is a poet, translator and journalist, a Fellow of the Royal Society of Literature and a Fellow of the Institute of Linguists.

ALISON BRACKENBURY was born in 1953. Her ninth collection is *Skies* (Carcanet, March 2016).

NEIL CURRY lives in Cumbria. His most recent collection of poems *Some Letters Never Sent* was published by Enitharmon Press. Last year Greenwich Exchange published his full-length study of William Cowper.

TONY CURTIS is Emeritus Professor of Poetry at the University of South Wales whose *New and Selected Poems: From the Fortunate Isles* is published by Seren in September 2016. This represents fifty years of writing and publishing. His selected stories *Some Kind of Immortality* are due from Cinnamon Press in 2017.

STEVIE DAVIES is Professor of Creative Writing at Swansea University. She is a Fellow of the Royal Society of Literature and a Fellow of the Welsh Academy. Stevie has published widely in the fields of fiction, literary criticism, biography and popular history. She has published books on Henry Vaughan, Milton, Donne and Shakespeare.

HILARY DAVIES is a poet, translator, essayist and teacher. Her fourth collection, *Exile and the Kingdom,* is due out from Enitharmon Press in autumn 2016. She has been a Gregory award winner, Hawthornden Fellow and Chairman of the Poetry Society, and is currently an RLF Fellow at King's College, London.

ANN DRYSDALE was born near Manchester, brought up in London, married in Birmingham, ran a small holding and raised three children on the North York Moors and now lives half way up a mountain in South Wales. She was a journalist for many years and wrote the longest-running by-line column for the *Yorkshire Evening Post.* She has published several poetry collections and non-fiction books and is joint editor of *Angle Journal of Poetry in English.* The poem from which she quotes in her piece is 'The Ram's Skull', from her collection, *The Turn of the Cucumber,* Peterloo Poets 1995. Anne Cluysenaar's diary poem, 'December 11 2010 – A Pekin Bantam' is from *Touching Distances* (Cinnamon Press), with kind permission.

KATE FOLEY is a widely published, prize-winning poet who has read in many UK and European locations. She lives between Amsterdam and Suffolk, where she performs, writes, edits, leads workshops and whenever possible works with artists in other disciplines. The Other Side of Sleep, awarded 1st prize by Jackie Kay in The Second Light poetry competition, is the title poem in a book of narrative poems published by Arachne Press, 2014 which in 2015 brought out her 8th publication, The Don't Touch Garden.

JAN FORTUNE was born in Middlesbrough and read theology at Cambridge. She completed a doctorate in feminist theology at Exeter University and has worked as a teacher, priest and charity director. She is the founding editor of Cinnamon Press and her previous publications include non-fiction titles in alternative education and parenting, as well as three poetry collections, most recently *Slate Voices* (a collaborative collection with Mavis Gulliver) and *Stale Bread & Miracles,* and three novels, *The Standing Ground, Dear Ceridwen* and *Coming Home.* She lives in the wild wet foothills of the Moelwyns in North Wales, beneath the abandoned slate village of Cwmorthin.

ROSE FLINT's fifth collection *A Prism for the Sun* (from Oversteps) explores personal relationship with the land and its creatures, particularly birds. One section also records some of Flint's responses to events and emotions experienced as a writer working in healthcare; notably during residencies at the Royal United Hospital, Bath and ten years with the Kingfisher Project in Salisbury District Hospital.

JOHN FREEMAN's *White Wings: New and Selected Prose Poems* appeared from Contraband Books in 2013. Previous collections include *A Suite for Summer* (Worple Press), and *The Light Is Of Love, I Think: New and Selected Poems* (Stride Editions). Stride also published a collection of essays, *The Less Received: Neglected Modern Poets.* He taught for many years at Cardiff University and lives in the Vale of Glamorgan. http://www.johnfreemanpoetry.co.uk/

PHILIP GROSS is a poet, winner of the T.S. Eliot Prize, as well as librettist and writer for young people. 2015 saw a new poetry collection, *Love Songs of Carbon,* and *A Fold*

CONTRIBUTORS

In The River, a collaborative exploration of the Taff Valley near Quakers Yard with artist Valerie Coffin Price. He is, coincidentally, a Quaker – and is Professor of Creative Writing at the University of South Wales.

DAVID GRUBB writes poetry, short stories and novels. Individual poetry collections have been published by Shearsman, Salt, Stride, Poetry Business and Like This Press. New work is due in 2017. He also teaches creative writing and creative reading courses.

GRAHAM HARRIS is secretary/treasurer of the Usk Conservation and Environmental Group. Anne was a valued and active supporter, and participated in walks, talks and discussions about how the Group could evolve and progress for the benefit of wildlife and conservation.

GRAHAM HARTILL worked for several years alongside Anne and Hilary Llewellyn-Williams as a poetry editor for *Scintilla*. He works as a writer in residence in HMP Parc, Bridgend and teaches on the MSc in Creative Writing for Therapeutic Purposes for the Metanoia Institute. 'Migrating Bones' also appears in *Scintilla 19*.

DAVID HART born in Aberystwyth, lives in Birmingham, has crossed between the Midlands and Wales in his poetry and so encountered Anne at gatherings of poets. His *Crag Inspector* (Five Seasons Press, 2002), a book-length long poem of Bardsey Island, was written for such a gathering, at the border Bleddfa Centre. His latest book, *Library Inspector, or The One Book Library* (Nine Arches, 2015), is set in Mid-Wales fantasised.

JEREMY HOOKER's most recent publications are: *Openings: A European Journal* (Shearsman) and *Scattered Light* (Enitharmon Press), his eleventh collection of poems since 1974. He has published extensively on modern British and American poetry, Welsh writing in English, the literature of landscape and place, and sacred poetry. His features for BBC Radio 3 include *A Map of David Jones*. He is Emeritus Professor of English at the University of South Wales and a Fellow of the Welsh Academy and of the Learned Society of Wales.

RIC HOOL's recent publications include *Selected Poems* (Red Squirrel Press 2013) and *A Way of Falling Upwards* (Cinnamon Press 2014). The first British publication of *Last Fair Deal Gone Down*, a docu-story conflating the lives of the author, seminal blues singer/guitarist Robert Johnson and Eric Clapton, originally published in *Fulcrum No. 6 (Annual of Poetry & Aesthetics) USA*, can be viewed on Junction Box 6: glasfrynproject.org.uk/w/category/junction-box/ A new collection of poems, *Between So Many Words*, is published by Red Squirrel Press, April 2016. He has organized the poetry reading series *Upstairs at the Hen & Chicks* in Abergavenny for the past 22 years. He is from Northumberland but lives in Wales.

JEREMY HILTON's poetry has appeared in magazines and anthologies, in the UK and worldwide, since the mid-1960s. He has had twelve collections published by the small presses, the most recent being *Lighting Up Time, New and Selected Poems* (Troubador Press, Leicester, 2007). He has also written three novels, the third of which,

A Sound Like Angels Weeping, was published by Brimstone Press in 2013. He writes regular reviews for *Tears In The Fence*, and in recent years has been composing contemporary chamber music – two String Quartets have been performed at Lauderdale House in North London. From 1995 to 2012 he edited and published the acclaimed poetry magazine, *Fire*.

ROGER HUBANK is an award-winning novelist whose work is largely devoted to exploring risk-taking in a wilderness of one kind or another. *Hazard's Way* won the Boardman Tasker Prize, the Grand Prix at the Banff Mountain Book Festival, and a special commendation from the Royal Society of Literature. *North* received a Special Jury award at the Banff festival. Other novels include *North Wall*, *Taking Leave* and *Evening Light*. Formerly Lecturer in English Literature at Loughborough University, his essays on William Blake and Denise Levertov have appeared in *Scintilla*. In November 2014 four of his novels were reissued in the United States.

JOHN KILLICK publishes poems, reviews and essays in a variety of magazines. He has recently edited volumes of selected poems by Anna Adams, Stanley Cook and Angus Martin for Shoestring Press. He has worked for over two decades as a writer with people with dementia and edited eight volumes of their verse. He has also published five books on communication and creativity in dementia, the most recent of which is *Dementia Positive* (Luath Press 2014).

STEVIE KRAYER's publications include three collections and an anthology, *A Speaking Silence: Quaker Poets of Today* (co-edited with R V Bailey). Her latest collection is *New Monkey* (Indigo Dreams, 2014). She lives in the Usk Valley in Wales with her husband, writer David N Thomas.

HILARY LLEWELLYN-WILLIAMS is the author of four collections of poetry from Seren, and lives in Abergavenny, S.E Wales. She worked for many years as a creative writing tutor, and was a colleague of Anne Cluysenaar at Cardiff University. She co-edited the poetry submissions for *Scintilla* with Anne and Graham Hartill for over ten years. She now works as a counsellor/psychotherapist in private practice, but still writes poems.

PAUL MATTHEWS teaches at Emerson College in Sussex. His two books on the creative process – *Sing Me the Creation* (now in its second edition) and *Words in Place* – are published by Hawthorn Press. *The Ground that Love Seeks* and *Slippery Characters* (Five Seasons Press) are gatherings of his poetry and most easily available from the author: Paulmatthewspoetry.co.uk

MARY MACGREGOR was born and brought up in the Valleys which she left when she went to Bristol University to study history. Subsequently she spent more than forty years teaching mainly English to the Anglo-Saxons in comprehensive schools in Essex. After her husband's death at the beginning of the millennium, she returned to live in Wales since when she has been under a compulsion to write poetry.

CONTRIBUTORS

PATRICIA McCARTHY, winner of The National Poetry Competition 2013, is the editor of *Agenda*. She is half Irish and half English. After Trinity College, Dublin, she lived in Washington D.C., Paris, Bangladesh, Nepal and Mexico. She has been settled for a long time in East Sussex. Recent collections are: *Rodin's Shadow* (Clutag Press), *Horses Between our Legs*, *Letters to Akhmatova* (2015). *Shot Silks* is due from Waterloo Press 2016. Her work has appeared in many journals and anthologies.

CHRISTOPHER MEREDITH is a novelist, poet and translator who lives in Brecon. Novels: *Shifts*, *Griffri*, *Sidereal Time*, *The Book of Idiots*. Poetry collections include *The Meaning of Flight* and *Air Histories*.

HELEN MOORE is an ecopoet and community artist/activist based in Somerset. Her debut collection, *Hedge Fund, And Other Living Margins*, was published in 2012 by Shearsman Books and was described by Alasdair Paterson as being "in the great tradition of visionary politics in British poetry." Her second collection, *ECOZOA*, which synthesises William Blake's 'Four Zoas' with Thomas Berry's vision of the Ecozoic Era, was published by Permanent Publications in 2015.

COLIN MOSS has a long-standing interest in poetry, the arts, and spirituality. Publications include essays on poetics in *Temenos Academy Review* and *Acumen*, and poems in *Scintilla* and other magazines. The proudest moment of his literary life was being awarded the *Scintilla* long poem prize by Anne, but the privilege of her friendship was a greater honour.

WENDY MULFORD's *And Suddenly, Supposing: Selected Poems*, containing most of her 13 small-press collections up to 2000, is still the definitive text for her early work. Recent collections since the SP include *The Land Between*, from Reality Street (2009) and, forthcoming, *The Stone: Poems from Orkney*. She divides her time between Suffolk & Orkney, where, from 2016, she will be converting a space for writers & artists (all kinds).

FRANK OLDING was brought up in Abertillery. He was educated at the universities of Cardiff, Leicester and Bristol and has lived in Abergavenny since the mid-1980s. He is an archaeologist by profession and works as Heritage Officer for Blaenau Gwent Borough Council. He writes in Welsh and is widely published as a poet and critic. He was Welsh-language editor of *Poetry Wales* from 1988-1995 and has helped run the Collective Press since 1990. He was adjudged joint second for the crown at the Bala National Eisteddfod in 2009. He was also poet in residence at the *Lle Celf* art exhibition at the Ebbw Vale National Eisteddfod in 2010 and is a member of the Gorsedd of Bards. His first collection, *Mynydd Du* ("Black Mountain"), was published by Gwasg y Bwthyn in 2012.

JAY RAMSAY is the author of 35 books of poetry, non-fiction, and classic Chinese translation. His latest publications are *Agistri Notebook* (KFS, 2014), *Monuments* (Waterloo Press, 2014), *Shu Jing – the Book of History* (Penguin Classics, 2014) and *Surgery* (Yew Tress Press, 2015) with *Dreams Down Under*, a sequence about Australia, forthcoming (KFS). He is also poetry editor of *Caduceus* magazine, and works in private practice as a UKCP accredited psychotherapist and healer, also running personal development workshops worldwide (www.jayramsay.co.uk.)

MYRA SCHNEIDER's most recent collection is *The Door to Colour* (Enitharmon 2014). She co-edited *Her Wings of Glass*, an anthology of ambitious poetry by contemporary women poets (Second Light Publications 2014). Other publications include books about personal writing. She tutors for The Poetry School in London and is consultant to the Second Light Network of Women Poets.

SEÁN STREET's ninth full collection is *Camera Obscura* (Rockingham Press), published in 2016, poems which explore the connection between voices across time and space. Recent prose includes *The Memory of Sound* and *The Poetry of Radio* (Routledge). Previous writings include books on Gerard Manley Hopkins and The Dymock Poets. He is Emeritus Professor at Bournemouth University.

NORMAN SCHWENK says one of his proudest achievements was to bring Anne Cluysenaar in to the Cardiff University teaching staff when the postgraduate Creative Writing programme was being set up in the early 1990s. This was the beginning of a firm friendship. In 2015 Norman celebrated his 80th birthday with a new collection of poems, *Book of Songs*, from Parthian Books. In 2016 Parthian plan to bring out his *Selected Poems*.

BONNIE THURSTON lives quietly in her home state of West Virginia, U.S.A, after spending many years as a university professor. She is a poet and author of numerous books on the New Testament and spirituality, the most recent being *Hidden in God: Discovering the Desert Vision of Charles de Foucauld*, 2016, Ave Maria Press. Her poem 'St. Melangell's Rabbits': Copyright 2011 by Order of Saint Benedict. Published by Liturgical Press, Collegeville, Minnesota. Used with permission.

DAVE WARD co-founded The Windows Project in 1976, running writing workshops in community venues and schools throughout Merseyside and the north west. His published work includes *Jambo* (Impact), *On The Edge of Rain* (Headland) and (as David Greygoose) *The Tree of Dreams* (HarperCollins) and *Brunt Boggart* (Hawkwood). Published in over 100 anthologies and broadcast on BBC TV and radio.

JOHN POWELL WARD is a Fellow of the Welsh Academy and former editor of *Poetry Wales*. Latest poetry collection was *The Last Green Year* (Cinnamon 2009); *Instead of Goodbye* (Cinnamon) is scheduled for 2017. Latest experimental poetry in *The Art of Typewriting* (Thames & Hudson 2015). Latest academic piece 'Wordsworth's legacy for the twentieth century poets' appeared in the *Oxford Handbook to William Wordsworth* (2015).

ALLAN AND HELEN WILCOX met as students of English at Birmingham University in the early 1970s, where they were taught by Anne. They both managed to keep literature at the heart of their careers, Allan as a teacher of English and Drama (as well as a freelance jazz musician) and Helen as a lecturer in English Literature. After extended periods of working in Liverpool and The Netherlands, they now live in Snowdonia, North Wales, where Allan continues as a jazz bassist and in his 'retirement' is a lay minister in the Church in Wales, while Helen is professor of English at Bangor University.

CONTRIBUTORS

ROBERT WILCHER was formerly Reader in Early Modern Studies in the English Department at the University of Birmingham and is now an Honorary Fellow of the university's Shakespeare Institute in Stratford-upon-Avon. His publications include *Andrew Marvell* (Cambridge, 1985), *The Writing of Royalism 1628-1660* (Cambridge, 2001), *The Discontented Cavalier . . . Sir John Suckling* (University of Delaware, 2006), and articles and chapters on Shakespeare, Quarles, Vaughan, Marvell, Milton, *Eikon Basilike*, Lucy Hutchinson, and various modern dramatists. He is currently one of a team of three working on a new edition of Henry Vaughan's works for Oxford University Press.

CHARLES WILKINSON's work includes *The Snow Man and Other Poems* (Iron Press) and *The Pain Tree and Other Stories* (London Magazine Editions). His recent poems have appeared in *Poetry Wales*, *Poetry Salzburg* (Austria), *The SHOp* (Eire), *The Reader, New Walk, Magma, Under the Radar, Tears in the Fence, Envoi, Orbis, Scintilla, The Warwick Review* and other journals. A pamphlet, *Ag & Au*, came out from Flarestack Poet in 2013. He first met Anne when he was an undergraduate at the University of Lancaster, but subsequently attended Trinity College, Dublin, her alma mater.

DILYS WOOD founded Second Light Network of Women Poets in 1994 and has co-edited six anthologies of women's poetry, the latest *Her Wings of Glass* (2014) and *Fanfare* (2015). She has two collections of poetry published and regularly co-edits ARTEMIS poetry magazine, a journal focused on women's poetry and written entirely by women.

THE ARTIST

Ann Johnson lives and works on the south coast of England. Her drawings and paintings have appeared in magazines and on covers of poetry books including *A Screen of Brightness* (Meredith Andrea and Fiona Owen) and *The Green Gate* (Fiona Owen). Her paintings have been selected on a number of occasions for the Royal Academy Summer Exhibition.
She says, 'I draw and paint what is around me: landscape, gardens, flowers, animals, treasured pieces of pottery. Through a range of media, I try to locate something of the integral nature of the subject.'
www.annjohnsonpaintings.net

The cover image is *Sleeping Garden*.

THE PHOTOGRAPHER

John Briggs was raised bilingually, studied French at university and, in 1974, came to Wales to do teacher training and teach French. Photography was also a passion and when he retired from teaching in 1999, he pursued it seriously. As well as having three photo-documentaries published by Seren, he has also specialised in photographing literary events, and that is how he came to photograph Anne at an open mic reading in Newport. He writes: 'On the night Anne read at the Murenger, in Newport, we had a good conversation, because she and I shared a common Belgian background'. With thanks to John for his kind permission for us to use his photograph.

Printed in Great Britain
by Amazon